SQUASH RACQUETS

The Khan Game

SQUASH RACQUETS

the Khan Game

by Hashim Khan
with Richard E. Randall

foreword: Arthur B. Sonneborn

current photographs: George Gellatly
diagrams: John C. Dunning

Wayne State University Press   *Detroit, 1967*

acknowledgements

The authors wish to thank Edward J. Hahn, Bruce G. Klaas, John C. Dunning, and Arthur B. Sonneborn for their painstaking review of the manuscript of this book, and their many valuable suggestions.

foreword

Whatever your relation to squash racquets, I believe you will enjoy Hashim Khan's book, and learn from it. If you are a beginner, it will give you a solid foundation for your game. If you are an advanced player, you will still find many clues for improvement. And even if you do not play, and have no intention of doing so, this book will add to your understanding as a follower and spectator of the sport.

You may be startled at first by the style of writing. Let me say in explanation that Hashim never learned to write English, or even to speak it, in textbook fashion. So he "talked" the book, in a great number of sessions, in the court and out of it, with Richard E. Randall, one of his students and a professional writer. The collaboration has worked well, I believe. The book gives you Hashim as he actually thinks and talks. It gives you his ideas on the game, *and* it gives you his personality.

Hashim has proved the soundness of his ideas conclusively. Since he entered national-level match play in India in 1944, he has established a record of victories that has no parallel in the game. What is generally considered the supreme test of the squash racquets player, the British Open, he won seven times, the last at the age of 42! No one has ever equalled this performance. His brother Azam won the British Open four times, and the great Egyptian amateur, F. D. Amr Bey, won it five times.

Herbert Warren Wind, one of America's most respected observers of the sports scene, said this about Hashim in the *New Yorker:* "The more I think about it, the more firmly convinced I am that the greatest athlete for his age the world has ever seen may well be Hashim Khan, the Pakistani squash player."

In a very real sense we owe Hashim's presence in the U.S., and the brilliance of American match play in recent years, to Edwin Hicks (Ned) Bigelow of New York. Mr. Bigelow was the major force in the establishment of the United States Open in 1954, which for the first time admitted professionals to top-level competition with our best amateurs. He was also instrumental in persuading the Khans, led by Hashim, to come to this country to play.

Hashim Khan has been blessed with good health, a keen mind, and phenomenally quick reactions. But if you read between the lines in his book, I think you will learn that what really has made him a champion is persistent practice, life-long self-discipline, and unbelievable determination.

We can't all be Hashim Khans, no. But those who adopt his principles of play, practice them, and build the will to win can go far in this wonderful game of squash racquets!

Arthur B. Sonneborn
March 31, 1967
Detroit, Michigan, U.S.A.

contents

photographs

diagrams

chapter 1

My Life — So Far

1

Greetings!

You buy this book to learn about squash racquets and my idea is to start the lessons for you on Page Number One.

"No," my friends say, "First tell about your life."

My life? This does not seem proper.

"When I go to my doctor with some pain, he does not tell me about his life first."

"Not the same thing," friend say, "You are no doctor, nobody has a pain. You are a champion of squash racquets, champions always tell about their life when they get old enough. You are old enough."

So it is you hear about my life first.

I am born in Nawakille, a village near city of Peshawar, Northwest Frontier Province, India, in 1916. All my people belong to Kalil Mohmund tribe of Pathans. They are Moslem, they believe in God very much, they are poor but they do not worry about this, and they are ready to put down their life for a friend.

I tell you about my tribe, for there are many other Pathans in this province — Yusafzais, Mahsuds, Darush Khel Waziris, others. These tribes live in mountains and no one tells them what to do. They do not live in law, British law or Indian law, they are very quick to fight.

But the Kalil Mohmunds, my tribe, come down from mountains a long time ago into flat land and they live in law.

Nawakille has maybe one thousand people, dirt streets, small houses, little gardens for vegetables, some chickens. It is a village for working people. In Nawakille, nothing much occurs.

But Peshawar, a big city you can find on your map, is close, and there many things happen. You walk fifteen minutes east from Nawakille, and you come into British cantonment where soldiers stay. Since my great, great grandfather, there are many many British soldiers in Peshawar, and they are there to keep watch on Khyber Pass, about forty miles away, in mountains. Nobody ever tries to come through this Pass.

These Englishmen are a long, long way from home. You think they are lonely? Yes, soldiers, perhaps. Officers, no I do not think. They have bat boys to run for them. With them they have their families, and it is not too difficult for their begums because they do not clean or cook: people of Nawakille come to do these things for a few rupees a month. And the Khyber Pass does not take all officers' time. In morning they have duty. After this they are free, and when the sun cools a little they go to their club to see what they can do.

At this club, the officers have many amusements: lawn tennis, hard racquets, squash racquets, billiards, swimming pool, drinking cocktails in bar. Two times every week there is music and they go dancing in ballroom. This club is not small: for one sport, lawn tennis, twenty-five courts!

My father, Abdullah Khan, is Chief Steward of this Club, an excellent position. He loves all sports, he is keen

16

tennis player. And he understands small boys, my father. When I start to walk to club from Nawakille to watch these games, he does not say No. Then, I am about 8 years.

Here I see squash racquets for first time.

2

I climb little steps in back wall of court and look down inside at this game. All walls are brick covered by plaster. Floor is cement. Ceiling? No ceiling, court is open to sky. This lets in light and air. Also, rain. When this occurs, British go inside to play cards or something amusing.

First time I sit on this back wall, no other boys sit with me. There is a mistake in game and ball flies out from top. But British officers do not run out little back door. They stand and look up to smile at me. I jump down outside and send the ball back in, quick. Four or five times ball flies out. Always I am glad to send it back. I wish this game to continue.

Next day is again like this. For me it is a good arrangement. I chase ball, this way I pay for my place on back wall. But officers do not understand, they think *they* must pay! Soon I have regular job, I come to courts every day after school to chase ball, and for this every month I receive five rupees, same as $1 American money. I have annas from my father before, but never rupees. I think I am rich!

In afternoon, late, maybe 5 o'clock, officers go to showers in clubhouse, they wish to make themselves clean for dinner. Then ballboys come down off wall and go in courts to play. I come down also. We play until we cannot see ball for reason it is dark. And sometime when moon is high and bright and shines in court, we continue to play long long time. You understand, there is no electric.

There is a difficulty. I am a very small boy with big racquet. I must put my hand high on handle to make my stroke. But I have a quick eye and I can run. I am so light I can run up and down court many games and never do I have a pain in my ribs. When it is my stroke and ball is a long way off, I run fast. When I run, it seems there is enough time always, time stretches out like some rubber band, and I am there for stroke. In this way I am fortunate.

During this time, I play lawn tennis also with my young friends. When it rains and there are no games outdoors, I watch officers play billiards inside. Delightful game! Later, when I am tall enough, I am permitted to take a cue in hand and play a little. I feel good in this club. The officers speak Pakhtu to me, this is Pathan language, and I also speak some English to them. A few words at this time. Not much. One can play games and never need much to talk, only to count. I learn English names for numbers very quick!

An accident occurs when I am eleven. My father makes everything ready for a tea party for the officers and their families at a steeplechase near Peshawar. He is on truck carrying all the flowers and sandwiches and punch. Driver makes a mistake and goes into a stone wall. My father flies from his seat and goes betwe n this truck and wall. In a moment he dies. I am on truck also and see this.

It is a sorry time for us, he is a good man, Abdullah Khan. He has four children: me, I am oldest, two sisters, and baby brother Azam. But we do not worry how we

18

will live. My mother receives a pension now from the club, and there is some money in our house. There is enough.

3

After my father dies, I begin to change from a little boy. I begin to think more. When I am twelve, I tell my mother, "I want to stop school and stay on squash courts all day."

Mother does not like this. "You are small boy," she says, "You must learn in school, you cannot get a man's job. You stop now, people think 'Those people are very poor, Hashim must chase balls to bring home a few rupees.' They will look down on us. We do not need money."

For a while I go to school, but it is like I am not there. I do not hear teacher, I do not see what it is he puts on blackboard. He thinks I am in his room, but I am in court, playing squash. I hear ball dash on wall, I see it bounce to me. I sit on floor in this school, yes, but my arm makes squash strokes.

It is wrong to be here in this school, I think. Nothing here helps me. But on courts, I can learn, someday I can make money this way. Look at professionals! English officers give them a salary to teach them game that comes from England. Yes, they play well, they work many years with this game, they start young. I must work now, too. If I wait four, five more years to finish school, I am too late for this sport.

I am a boy, yes, but I see few good jobs for my people. A little education does not help. If you can go to

19

be a doctor or a lawyer in a university in England, excellent, yes! But who in Nawakille has money for this?

So I stop school, never I go back. But I do not make my mother sad other ways. I do not stop my religion. Every day I go to mosque in Peshawar to take instructions in Koran.

4

Now I have morning time free and there are squash courts empty at club. Sometimes I have no opponent, no ball boy is there so early. What do I do?

One thing, I play Hashim against Hashim. I stand in back and stroke ball very soft to front. True, that other Hashim knows where ball is going, I cannot keep this secret from him. Still he runs like a hare to arrive before second bounce. Ah, he succeeds! He drives ball hard and it flies to back. Now first Hashim must turn and run like a hare also, to be in time. So I turn to back, to front, to left side, to right side, always running, stroking, running, stroking.

One day an officer comes to top of wall and watches. "Young man," he says. "You kill yourself." I do not like to worry this man. I slow down until he goes away.

It is good to run as hard as you can like this. You find out what you can do. Then you play a real opponent and never touch your limit, you are surprised, everything is more easy. But I do not know these reasons when I am a boy. I play alone because I am alone, that is all.

One way to learn fast, I know, is lessons, but one does not arrange this in a moment. Not every ball boy has a teacher. When my father is alive, he is a good friend of

Abdullah Majid Khan, head coach for squash racquets at British Club. He wears a beard, he is old, and is very busy with officers. I do not like to ask him: it is not proper for such an important man to take time with a ball boy.

But Abdullah Majid has a son, Ismathullah, he is assistant, maybe 25 years, no beard. Also, he makes jokes, and he is very good in court. Before he come to work for his father, he is professional for Viceroy of India in Delhi.

One morning I say to Ismathullah, "Give me a lesson, and I give you four annas." This is my lunch money and is the same as 5c. I am lucky this day. Ismathullah needs this money.

We go into court and play ball back and forth. Ismathullah keeps close watch. "You stroke too late," he says. "Your body is too close to ball." Such things. I want to show him how I run. He does not care to see me run, there is enough wrong when I am standing in one place.

Many lessons I have from this man. Always I give him something, a little money, some fruit, to show him thanks. Many times Ismathullah says, "No, I want nothing."

I work alone also. Not running only. One thing I want is to make ball move properly to some mark. I stand in one place in court and make same shot many many times. Maybe one hundred, two hundred times. When ball begins to go again and again to that certain place where I aim, I go to a new position and I start again. Almost every day I do this. After a while, it is like court moves inside my head, I can close my eyes and see everything. Eyes shut, I stroke and ball goes to that mark.

All time I go to club in these years, I grow and get strong in arm and wrist. My racquet feels more light,

21

When I am boy, 16, I go with friends to play hard racquets for British Officer's Club, Rawalpendi. 1932 is one very good year for Rawalpendi. Look at cups!

I move my hand down on handle. I learn to snap my wrist and send ball like a bullet.

My lessons begin to change. They are not lessons, they are games. This does not happen all at once, this change. I do not remember when — maybe I am sixteen — when Ismathullah says nothing about mistakes. He puts all his thinking on his play, he does not relax, he runs and strokes hard and works for points. I go into court with him like I am opponent.

Now some British officers watch me in courts with Ismathullah and other friends, and they begin to say, "Give me a game, please, Hashim." I am delighted.

Soon I do not sit on back wall to watch for ball flying out. I am not a ball boy. I am a squash player!

5

When I go into court with some officer, I do not say, "Keep eye on ball," "Bend down for strokes," "Snap wrist," things like that. This is not proper, I am not a professional.

Still, I do not give them what one calls "Customer's Game." True, I put ball where they can reach it when they run fast, and many times I make out that I cannot reply to their stroke. I give them a close game. This way they think maybe next time, they beat me. This is good. If you beat a man bad, you keep him without a score, then he has no hope, never he wants to go in court with you again. This makes me feel sorry, too. It is not good sport.

Yes, I play but I do not coach. At this time there are professionals enough in Peshawar. No club needs one more. But I do not wish to leave home. I have patience, I wait, I am still young. I earn a little money stringing racquets with new gut and for being a playing partner on the courts. I do not need money for smoking or drinking, I am Moslem, and also a single man.

My good friend Safirullah Khan is also a young squash player who waits. He is another son of Abdullah Majid Khan, but Ismathullah is already Assistant, there can be no place for Safirullah. We never worry. We play and wait. This life we choose.

Soon baby brother Azam is no baby, he walks to club from Nawakille, he is a ball boy, and I begin to show him different games I know. I am surprised, he likes lawn tennis best.

When he is 22 Safirullah marries my sister and now he waits in Peshawar no more. They go to Lucknow in India, where he is professional in a British cantonment, then they go to Waziristan, then Karachi.

While I wait in Peshawar, Safirullah has son, name of Mohibullah Khan, and this son becomes a champion of squash racquets later. After while, I tell you about this boy.

One day in 1942 everything changes. The commander of British Air Force in Peshawar, walks to our club to play tennis with Abdullah Majid. While they are on court, the commander says, "Our professional is leaving, who is a good man for us?" Abdullah Majid answers, "Hashim Khan, I know him well."

So it is I become tennis and squash professional for Air Force Officer's Mess: a man leaves, another man speaks my name. It is luck for me, and I am very happy I do not wait longer. I am 28 years old.

Fifty rupees a month I get in this job! With such money one can marry and raise a family. This I do. In this same year, I marry Mehria, a girl of my village. This is arranged by my mother a long time before, and we go to live in my mother's house in Nawakille. This is custom in my country.

My job is most pleasant. In mornings, I give lessons to officers, they make appointments with me when they have time free from duty in Air Force planes. In afternoon, I do not give lessons. I go in courts with officers and play, play, play until they are tired out, and go to showers. Also I play professionals so I will not forget to run and work.

Where is a better job? I hope I have this life in Peshawar forever.

6

One day—it is 1943—a gentleman, name of Mr. Sine —I never see him before—comes to me at Air Force courts

24

to say, "Where is Abdullah Majid? He is not at Army Club. I am finished with my business in Peshawar and I wish to play squash with him."

"He is gone to the mosque for prayer and cannot be disturbed," I say, "but if you wish, I play you."

"I wish to play with professional," Mr. Sine says and I reply, "I am a professional."

"No," he says, "I am sure I will have a good game with Abdullah Majid, I am waiting for him."

Not often I become angry, this is one time. "I will give you one game," I say, "and start myself with *minus fifty points*." Mr. Sine looks at me like I am a crazy man and says, "What, you give me a fifty point handicap? Abdul Bari, he is best in India, he gives me thirty points, and you give me fifty?"

I am surprised. Abdul Bari is my cousin, he comes from my village, but he goes away early. He is top professional at Bombay Cricket Club and everybody says, no one takes a game from Abdul Bari.

I say again, this time more soft. "Yes, fifty points!" I cannot change handicap now, I lose face this way. Mr. Sine makes loose his tie and looks around. "Where do I change clothes?" he says.

I find out in court, he is keen player. Also, he is in good condition. He runs well. For reason I have 59 points to make, he has 9 only to make to win, I cannot take too many chances with kill shots: maybe I hit tin! So I take care. We play long rallies. After while Mr. Sine does not run so well, I make points more quick. I win, yes, but for this one handicap game we are in court near one half hour!

Mr. Sine is gentleman. He puts hand out to shake when he goes, and he laughs and says. "Please tell Abdullah Majid already I have good game." Now I am sorry I am angry with him. I tell myself never I give such handicap like this another time. I keep cool.

Later, I find out Mr. Sine is Manager of Granley Bank in Bombay, also he is number two amateur squash player in this city!

7

Next year, Bombay Cricket Club starts a big squash match — All-of-India it is called — and players from everywhere in country, professionals, amateurs, have chance to try for this new championship.

Abdullah Majid says, "Go and try, Hashim."

"Too many good players," I reply.

"You do not need to give a fifty point handicap," he says.

I do not believe he knows about my game with Mr. Sine. Never I tell anyone. He laughs to see surprise in my face.

"Go and try," says Abdullah Majid.

The Air Force Commander is polite when I ask him for time to go to Bombay. "Yes," he says, "if it is all right with my staff." I believe he thinks this is like going for a holiday, something for me only. He does not see what I try to do for Peshawar when I am in Bombay.

Never do I play inside on wood courts before, always on cement, so I take train to Bombay two days early to learn how ball bounces from wood. Then I am ready.

In Peshawar there is no comfortable room for people to watch game. In courts in Bombay, they have a gallery, and for first time, I am in front of many people watching: officers, officials of government, newspaper writers, photographers. Mr. Sine, he is there also.

I am not nervous, I think only what I must do with ball. Gallery is back of me. But sometimes I turn. When there is a good rally and I win, when my opponent takes a point with a clever shot, people become excited and clap the hands. Then I must turn and watch this gallery. I like people to be happy in this game.

Three matches I play, then it is finals, and my opponent is a man I never see since we are boys in Nawakille, my cousin Abdul Bari.

We play. Now Abdul Bari has best soft drop shot I see anywhere. This is how he makes points. But I am light like a fly, 112 pounds only, and never before does he see me run. I watch him close. When I see him start with wrist to make that drop shot, that moment I am on way to front. He thinks I am never in time, he relaxes. Abdul Bari is relaxing still when I reach and stroke and put that ball away. He is a big man, heavy man, and many times he does not move fast enough to make a reply. This is how I come out ahead.

Pictures and stories are in papers right away and quick the news goes home that RBAF squash professional in Peshawar goes to Bombay and wins All-of-India first time they play this match. When I get off train, my officers are there, they laugh and pound me all over and say, "Good Fellow!" "Congratulations!" — such things. In the mess, commander shakes hands with me. "You bring honor to our group," he says, and staff gives me a gift of money for train ticket and all expense in Bombay. "Of course, you must defend this title next year," the commander says.

Quite right. In 1945 and in 1946 again, I return to Bombay for All-of-India. But not in 1947, nobody thinks

27

of big sports competition this year, this is when we have Partition.

You hear about Partition? This is when my country begins. I am always Pathan, yes, I belong to these people, but now many different people come together, and we have our new country, not India — Pakistan. We have our government, soldiers, Air Force, we are members of British Commonwealth.

British begin to leave, officers I know for many years, my old commander, they leave and go home to England. But Pakistan keeps English games. Also my job I keep and brother Azam's job, he is now tennis coach with me at officer's mess. We have always less and less British in courts with us, always more Pakistanis, and now we are working for Royal Pakistani Air Force, and we have a new commander, name of Kelly. He is an Irishman who stays a while until RPAF has some more experience.

This is a bad time for sports, Pakistani military is very busy for many months because of religious troubles. Hindus in Pakistan are unhappy to be under our law, and Moslems outside Pakistan are unhappy to be under Indian law. Hindus inside Pakistan try to get out, Moslems in India try to get in, and there is much fighting and killing, some in Peshawar. You can understand, no big sports matches are permitted.

In 1949 people are quiet enough. But I do not enter All-of-India, I am Indian no more. That is all right, we have our own games. Clubs from all over our country put together a match in squash racquets for all professionals. It is played in Kakul and I have honor to win this championship of Pakistan year it begins.

My opponent in finals is Roshan Khan, 21 years, son of sister of Safirullah, my brother-in-law. He belongs

28

to family, and I call him "cousin." Roshan is professional at Army Mess in Rawalpendi. His daddy and grandfather Abdullah Majid, they are professionals also. They teach him this game from time he is very small boy. Roshan is very fast, quick to think. He is fine stroke player, and he has lovely volley drop shot.

In this year, 1949, I am 33 years. Not young. But I am not too late. I make good name in this game, I have a good job, I have three children already. Maybe I am good for two-three more years of big match play in Pakistan, then young professionals can run for me, I stay and coach on Air Force courts. I can run with officers until I am old man. This is how I think about my life in future.

Now I tell you what happens.

8

In 1950 India sends Abdul Bari to London to try for world championship in English Open matches. He loses in finals, in close games with Mahmoud El Karim, champion of Egypt. That is all right, Abdul Bari brings a good feeling for India in papers and radio.

High Commissioner for us, Habib Rahmatullah, he goes to see Abdul Bari before he leaves London. "We have no player," he says, "You are Pakistani, come to live again in your country and next year come to England to try for us." Abdul Bari has an excellent job in Bombay Cricket Club in India, he says, "Sorry, no."

Now Brigadier Engle goes to High Commissioner and says, "Send Hashim Khan." Brigadier Engle, a British officer who retires and goes home to England, is Commandant of Military Academy in Kakul before and sees me play in matches for Pakistani championship. "Send Hashim Khan," he says, "He will be a credit to you." Habib Rahmatullah is a High Commissioner, a squash player no, he thinks, "Who is Hashim Khan?"

So he writes a letter to government in Karachi to ask, "Is Hashim Khan best man for us?" Government does not know. It sends a letter to military headquarters. *They* do not know, and one day question comes in mail to Commander Kelly. *He* does not know. He is old and never he plays squash.

So he tells me, "Hashim, play some games with good players and I watch and see if you go to London." So I give an exhibition with Pakistani professionals. Commander Kelly watches very close and after I come out of court, he says, "I see English matches before when I am in London, and I do not think you can win."

Group Captain Raza watches also, he sees me play many times and he comes to see what Commander Kelly does, and he says, "Hashim beats Abdul Bari many times and Abdul Bari plays in finals in London. Your staff thinks Hashim is a good man for Pakistan."

Commander Kelly is head man, yes, but this question is not about aeroplanes. They talk back and forth and then he says to Captain Raza, "If you wish, we send Hashim."

Nobody asks *me* do I want to go! I am not sorry to stay home. "El Karim is 30, I am 35 — too old perhaps for English Open," I say. "Too old to play for Pakistan?" asks Captain Raza. "No, I will go," I say. Captain is a quick thinker.

New government has no experience with such things, and no one thinks to put money in treasury to send a squash player to London. Still, they find enough for plane ticket. Then my officers in Air Force Mess give in what they can from their pay and soon there is $1,000 kitty, and I have some little money, and this is enough. Nobody hopes to get all money back. The world championship prize is 50 pounds, about $150. One plays this game for sport and honor.

9

First I fly to Edinburgh, it is custom in this time to play in Scottish Open before the English matches in London. I am most fortunate, I stay in these matches straight through, and in the finals in these two cities, my opponent is Mahmoud El Karim.

I do not see El Karim play until we come together in court, but I hear much. Nobody thinks I win, I have not any hope myself. I am not nervous, I will play like I play, I am not going to beat myself. But I have much respect for Mahmoud El Karim. He does much for himself. He is top professional in Gezira Sports Club in Cairo. He is world champion.

Never before do I see a man like this in squash racquets. He is higher than six feet, long arms and legs, and he moves about court like I see dancer in ballet, soft and smooth, you never hear his feet on floor, and how he turns and runs and strokes, you want to watch all day, it is wonderful. He is what one calls a stroke player, his play has rhythm, no jerks. And he has many many different shots, some I see for first time anywhere.

My game is simple at this time. I drive very hard and low, cross court, and sometimes I play soft drop shots, that is all. But speed on my feet I have this, I can get to ball. Also, I think fast. When I am up front in court and El Karim tries to pass me with ball, sometimes I surprise him: I do not run after that ball to back, I leap out and get that ball in front. Ball is going very fast, yes, but I see that ball clear, I have time to think about this ball and where I must leap and where I must place it. A newspaper man afterwards says I have a fast reflex, but is not a reflex like when you tap your knee, your leg jumps up? What I am telling you is not like this. My leg does not know what it does. I know what I do, and I give thanks for this gift, fast thinking.

When games are finished a British professional, tells me, "Many times you play off wrong foot." Quite right. This is when I must stroke in an instant. If I turn to face side wall, ball does not wait for me. I know it is not proper, it is bad style, it is not nice to see, it is a mistake. But sometimes it wins points.

After matches, there are banquets for all players and friends and officials. In Edinburgh, I never see this before, they put dining tables right in courts, musicians go in another court to play for us, and people keep lifting their glass to me and saying, "Your health, Champ!" In London, we are in a hotel and it is more serious. El Karim is there and we talk a little. He tells me he returns next year. King Farouk of Egypt sends him a telegram saying, "Do not worry Mahmoud, better luck next time."

10

Before I leave London, Habib Ramitullah says, "Pakistan is pleased by way you play, wait and you will see." He tells me, still I am surprised. When I land in plane at Karachi, Governor General and his officials come close to greet me. They give me a party and make speeches and I receive an excellent gold watch with engraving. This watch I still have. I cannot make a speech, all I can say is "Thanks!"

Then I fly in a special RPAF plane to Peshawar. There is a reception at airport with five hundred guests and then I am in an open car riding slow through city and every sidewalk is full of people waving, and there are many children because Chief Minister closes all schools this day I come home.

Never I think a squash player can have so much honor. Many people who come to see me are very poor, they never go inside English clubs, they always think before squash is perhaps an English soft drink, not some

My city Peshawar gives me big welcome, 1950, when I come home from British Open. Never I think squash player can have so much honor.

Melbourne, Australia 1951. You see bad form here, one leg in air. Sometime player must stroke quick—no time for proper position.

game. Still they come. They think I do something good for Pakistan and it helps make them glad to be Pakistani. They want to show me thanks.

Can I stop now? No, it is impossible, I must try again if Pakistan tells me. I hope they tell me. Yes, I play for my country, quite right. Also I play for myself and my family.

I return to London for '51 matches and again I meet Egyptian Mahmoud El Karim in finals.

After this match I go to play exhibition matches for Pakistan in Australia and New Zealand. Never do I play so much squash in so many places! I play fifteen, sixteen people every day, professionals, amateurs, when I am in

34

court with one, many others wait outside to be next. Every night I get in RPAF plane and fly to some other town, sleep a little and in morning go in court again. One week, I play three hundred fifty games! Soon I must put plaster on my fingers, and my shoulder hurts so I cannot raise my arm for proper stroke. But I do not wish to say, "Excuse me from game, I cannot stroke properly." I continue. Many friends I make in this country, and newspapers say I am good ambassador for Pakistan. I am glad to hear this. This is idea of matches, to make more people think good about my country.

When I go back home, I discover I am gazetted lieutenant in RPAF, with good officer's pay and life-time pension when I retire. Group Captain Raza helps to do this. It is not easy for him. I am a squash player, I cannot operate an aeroplane. Also I have no education. But a new job is made, lieutenant instructor in squash and tennis at new RPAF school in Risalpur, and President signs my commission. He says, "This is not proper, but we do this for Hashim."

This lieutenant instructor job is very easy. Nobody says, "You must be at academy so many hours or so many days" or "You must live in this place or that place." They say, "Do what you wish." So I buy motor scooter and two-three days every week, in one hour I ride scooter to Risalpur to give some few lessons to young men who study to fly, then I ride back home to Peshawar. When I am there in Risalpur, they do not permit me to spend money. My food is free. Also, I have a bat boy, no charge, who cares for my laundry and room.

They have other sport instructors, civilians, at Risalpur, they can teach everybody these games without me. I see they make up this commission of lieutenant to

35

give me more money and a pension when I am too old to play. It is a good thing for me. Already I have five children and more money is welcome.

You understand why I must always try now in big matches for my country? Anyway, I am very glad to do this as long as I can.

I fly to England third time for Open. In finals I meet Englishman, amateur, H. B. P. Wilson. Strong player! I win again . . . but I know not forever can I stay in courts with young men in the British Open. Soon somebody else must be ready to win for Pakistan.

11

Young brother Azam, he is tennis coach at RPAF Officer's Mess — is only 27. I say to him, "You want to go to England with me and play squash in Open Matches?" He says, "I am not good enough for squash, tennis is my game." I say, "We will see."

That summer '52 we go in court together every day. First day, we play one game, and before it is finished, Azam says, "Stop, you are killing me." I make him run very hard. But he comes back next day, and he goes two games. Next day, three games. Soon he is in good condition for this game, and we play hard two hours every day. Four or five months we play like this, and then I know Azam is ready. We go to England together for the '53 matches.

In London, Squash Racquets Association tells me, "We never see Azam play, we cannot permit him to enter." It is true, they have places for only sixteen players from every place in the world, they must know they are best.

"Try him," I say. So they put him in court with B. C. Phillips, one of best British amateurs, and Azam takes three games straight without difficulty. Association tells me, "Yes, he is permitted to enter."

I am very glad Azam is with me because I am sick with influenza before these '53 matches. London weather perhaps. Dr. Peter Holding Smith, he is British amateur squash champion at this time, comes to look at me and says, "You are too weak to play, stay off court." "I have come a long way," I say. "And I want to play." So Doctor Smith gives me an injection and some medicine.

In court, one moment I am hot with fever, next moment I have chills, but I can still play. I think perhaps I meet El Karim again, but he twists his knee in first round in games with Dr. Smith. I go through three rounds, and who is my opponent in finals? Young brother Azam! I am glad for reason even I lose, Pakistan wins! Azam loses this time, but later he wins World Championship four times!

12

Soon two more players go to London for Pakistan. There is Roshan Khan, my cousin, 12 years younger, he goes in '54. I tell you about him before. And for '56 matches, there is Mohibullah Khan, 17 years old, son of my old friend and brother-in-law Safirullah. All summer before '54 matches I play with Mohibullah on courts in Peshawar, then he flies with me to England to play. No, he does not win right away, he needs some experience, but when he is 24, this young man wins an Open title!

For a long time I think of my sons in this game. Can

they not also become coaches and make a living?

But I begin to have another idea. In 1954, after Open Match, I tour England with Roshan Khan, playing exhibitions wherever they ask us. We do this for money. One place we go is very nice private school in Somerset, and after games, headmaster asks me questions.

"You have boys?"

"Yes, three."

"Who is oldest?"

"Sharif, 11."

"Do you teach him this game?"

"Yes."

"Does he play well?"

"For a boy, yes."

"Better than other boys?"

"Yes."

"You like to send him to school here?"

I have to laugh, I know how much this costs.

"Send him," this headmaster says, "I take him with no charge."

I cannot believe it! An English education without charge?

More talk. I begin to believe it. My name is a long time in newspapers, many English people know it. It is good for school when son of Hashim Khan goes there to learn. People come to watch him play, perhaps. They write stories if he wins. Perhaps some daddies say, "I send my boy into this school, he will get a good education and good sports."

So Sharif goes to Somerset. He does not want to go. He knows not one word in English, only Pakhtu, and he cries for a long time in this school. It is not like going to club from Nawakille. He is 12,000 miles from home in

After British Open matches, 1955, Prince Philip presents cup. He is a
good squash player and has a court for himself at Buckingham Palace.

Nawakille. But then he learns after while he can be happy
in Somerset, and he learns English properly and studies
well, and also, he goes in courts. He does not make headmaster sorry. Before he leaves this school, he wins many
matches and two British Junior Amateur Championships.

Thirty-nine I am when Sharif goes first to Somerset
in '55—old yes, for a match player—but now I have

another reason to try again in England. I want to see my son.

13

A player with this many years does not run like before. But he gets experience. He plays many thousand games, he knows many things to do. Experience is not as good as to be young — there is nothing that good — but anyway I give thanks for it.

Early same year, '55, I am fortunate to win British Open sixth time, and after matches there is a cocktail party and Prince Philip of England is there to present cup to me. Prince Philip is a good player and has a court for himself in Buckingham Palace. We have a little talk.

"I do not play squash anymore," he says. "I am 35, too old." "Too old? I am 40," I say. "Yes," Prince Philip says, "You are pretty old and you have quite a tummy there, I am surprised you win today." He is quite right, I am 140 pounds — not good for 5'4" squash player. Then he laughs. "You still think fast enough," he says, "and I hope you come back."

I come back in '56, yes, but I have bad luck. I am playing cousin Roshan in finals, I win first game 9-6, we play second game and, all in one moment, I cannot run. Shin muscles in my two legs become very tight. I am like a car with brakes pushed down hard. Three games in a row I lose (9-5, 9-2, 9-1) and Roshan Khan is winner for Pakistan.

In '57 I enter again and win British Open seventh time with brother Azam in finals. Forty one years old I am!

I do not tell you before, but Azam for couple years stays in England, he is professional at *New Grampian's*, sports club in West London. In this club, people can sit at table and look down into courts with cocktail in hand. Also, there is billiards, badminton, and token machines (like slot machines in U.S.). This year, '57, owner says, "I am tired, you take this business." Quite right. Azam takes business and brings his family to London. I am happy. Son Sharif now has fine uncle to visit when he has holiday from school in Somerset.

In 1959 I go for last time to England to try in Open. This time I am in court in semi-finals with brother Azam, when I twist my knee quick-turning to stroke ball. Again, I cannot run. Azam wins this match, wins finals against cousin Roshan, wins his first World Championship for Pakistan!

I am 43 years in this last match. At such an age, the English Open is difficult. Experience helps to beat opponents, but it is not enough. Opponents in this match are best players anywhere, and I must try more every year to win. Wind stays good, yes, but you push too hard, and you have accidents with legs.

Better, I say to self, I stay away from Open. That is all right. I am not young when I start, and still I am lucky to win seven times. Also, I play this English game many places for Pakistan. I give exhibition in many small places in England, Scotland, New Zealand, Australia, India. I play in Egypt and Hong Kong. Also I play American game in Canada and United States.

Another reason I say enough to English matches, is now Pakistan has more players. I begin alone, but now there is Roshan and Azam and young Mohibullah. There are three from Pakistan in Canadian Open in Montreal in 1955—me and Roshan and Azam and we finish one, two, three. Canadian Minister of Education, he makes presentation of cup at banquet, he laughs and says, "This is Canadian Open but where in world are Canadians?"

41

When I think to quit English game after 1959, I have idea maybe I can last few more years of matches in America and Canada.

14

Before '54 English Open I go first time to United States for reason just I like to see American people and cities. But not real holiday. Pakistan ambassador makes arrangement for exhibition match in Philadelphia with Diehle Mateer, Jr., he is number one seeded U. S. player.

I have quick to make some change in Philadelphia. American court is more small than English, ball flies more fast, so player does not need to run so far to make get. Good for me, I like this. But I have trouble to know exact spot where ball is. Sometimes I think that ball is near front knee, right place for hit. I am wrong. Already it is behind me! I lose some points like this, so I speed my stroke and it goes better.

Couple days later I go to New York City to try in first U. S. Open. I lose in finals to small, quick player from Boston, Henry Salaun. But later I have some good match wins in U. S. and Canada. I meet excellent players, good sportsmen like Mr. Mateer and Mr. Salaun also Al Chassard, Ray Widelski, Sam D. Howe III. Plenty more. Then Azam and Roshan and Mohibullah come to play American game, also and I go in courts with them!

In 1955 I come to America second time, to try. I meet for first time my very good dear friend, Mr. Arthur Sonneborn. He is business man in Detroit. He loves this game of squash racquets, and comes to New York City to see U. S. Open. It is after quarter finals I think, he comes to locker room to introduce self.

He says to me, "I stand in gallery and watch you play. Sometime you cannot get to ball for reason opponent is in way, still you do not call for 'let.' You must ask for 'let' otherwise most times they never give it. Do not be afraid. Turn around to referee and say, loud, 'let'!"

Now he tells me, I understand something. In

Watch close your opponent to catch his idea soon as can. Opponent you see is Ed Hahn, owner of Detroit club where I am professional. Very strong player. Two times he wins U.S. Amateur championship.

English match game, referee is always professional squash player, he goes to school to study this job, they pay him to referee. He is boss. When something occurs in play, that instant, he calls out, loud. "Point!" or "Let!" or "Let Point!" or "Play!" Such things, whatever is proper. Player does not need to worry, does he get "let" or not. Referee decides.

In American game, one time in ten, maybe, you see professional referee. Referees are amateur. They do not ask money. It is like hobby. Referee like this not many times calls "let." First he lets player call "let" then he decides, "Yes, let!" or "No let." In 1955, I do not understand this and sometimes I think I need "let." Referee says nothing and I have idea maybe he cannot see problem. Not this man's fault, I see now. Just custom in America.

Mr. Sonneborn is good to help me like this. He sees I am new man in his country, and need friend!

I see him in America and Canada and England few times after 1955. Then, in 1960, I am home in Peshawar Pakistan, I am going to Risalpur to give lessons at RPAF Academy, and I receive a message from U. S.

It is from Mr. Sonneborn. He is secretary of a new sports club in Detroit, *Uptown Athletic Club*, and owner is Mr. Edward Hahn, an excellent player, two times U. S. Amateur Champion.

15

Mr. Sonneborn says, "Come to be professional at our club and we send you to play matches and exhibitions anywhere you want." It is a good offer, much more money than I make in Risalpur.

For some days I do not know what answer I give. What does my country think when I go? They do me much honor. Top men, yes, even President, they greet me like friends. I have no education, that is all right, they make me lieutenant anyway and give me easy job. They give me many gold medals, one time 10,000 rupees, another time some acres of land near Karachi. They put my name on a railroad station near Nawakille: it says "Hashim Khan's Village." Before I play for Pakistan, few people in my country know me. Now, many, many.

But I think: I do something good for Pakistan, also. It is in record. I can go and record stays. And when I go it is not like young player with many wins left, going. I am 44.

And United States I like. People I like, and also American game is more easy for my age. I have better chance with young men in match play.

What makes my decision, go or stay, is my family most of all. If I am alone with my wife, certainly I stay in my country. But I already have ten children, seven boys, three girls, and since Sharif goes to Somerset in '55, I think much how I can get proper education for everybody else.

You think perhaps these boys like squash racquets like daddy? Quite right. Not Sharif only. There is Gulmast, 16, and Aziz, 14, and Liaqat, 11, and Salim, 9, they all go in court and play. Two more boys, too small yet. I say to them, "Sharif is learning to be a chartered accountant, Gulmast is perhaps an engineer, good idea you all learn something to do for a living. Squash racquets you play well yes, but it is not idea for whole life. This is dangerous."

You understand, I give thanks for my life. I am very

45

fortunate to play game well and to have health all time. Over forty years I play, a few times I have fever or pull a muscle, but only four-five days do I stay off courts because I am sick. Can my sons have such luck? If a professional has an injury in his knee, and is off courts for three months, what does he do? All he knows is this game, he cannot make money. But if one has an education, he can have this same injury, and still he works, he does not need legs for his brain.

This is how I decide to go to United States. I tell Captain Raza and quick he gets papers signed for my resignation from RPAF. I tell my family soon they will come and I leave Nawakille and Peshawar to take this new job in Detroit.

It is eight years now I am in Detroit. All this time I give lessons at my club, I play in exhibitions in many cities. Still I go in match play in this country and Canada.

This is story of my life—so far.

How long can I play? My uncle Seid Ali Khan in Nawakille is 87 and he goes in squash court every day still. I am only 52. I continue.

Now we start lessons!

This is the first time I teach and do not see student. I do not know if you are a fat man, thin, tall, short like me, 60 years old, 20 years old. Maybe you are a woman. It makes no difference, welcome!

I have idea you do not know this game at all and I start at beginning. If I make a mistake and you are a squash player already, please have patience, I catch up to you later.

Let us go in court and close door and begin!

46

chapter 2

Beginning Things

court

Look in this court, you see why many people do not come to watch this game of squash racquets like boxing, tennis, such sports. Where do they go? They see a big box, walls every side, ceiling on top, little door to go in and out, and only a small place in back, high, for some seats.

One time I play in Heliapolis Club in Cairo, Egypt, they have galleries up high, all around, maybe 500 people sit down: biggest in world I think. Another court like this is in Philadelphia, belongs to University of Pennsylvania, but not so many seats. Lansdowne Club in London has gallery on two sides of court, room for maybe two hundred fifty to watch World Championship matches.

But many like this I do not see anywhere. Not money enough to build. Most courts I see, maybe fifty people squeeze to watch game.

But that is all right. Walls keep people out, yes, but they give joy to game. You thank these walls, I think. You play tennis, the ball goes by and you are not ready, too bad, you lose that point. In squash racquets not so always. Many times when you turn, you see back wall catch that ball and bounce it back to you. Maybe then you are ready. You have second chance.

In this court you see red stripes on floor and walls to tell you where is out of bounds, put foot in here to serve,

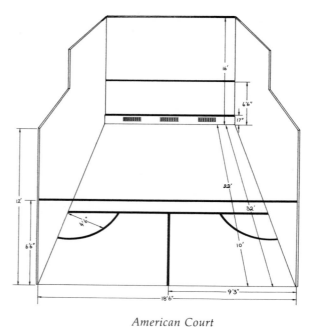

American Court

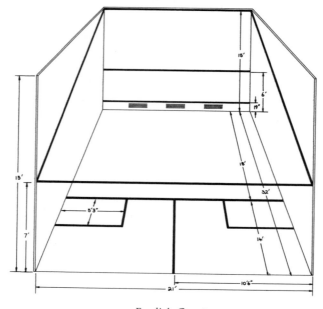

English Court

48

such things. You see them in pictures of courts, English court, American court, on facing Page. I want you to have the right court for your country. Not much difference. Big differences you see is English court is 2½ feet more wide than American court. You live in London you run more than Detroit.

idea of game

You go in the court with your opponent, he hits ball, you hit ball, he hits ball, each time you hit you see what you can do so this opponent does not return ball properly. This is idea of game. Sometimes you have problem in beginning. Two opponents. Other man and self!

Rules say only one bounce on the floor between strokes. Also, ball must go to front wall before it goes to floor. Yes, it can bounce on other walls before this, this is good squash, but front wall it *must* reach, higher than tin!

This *tin* (other name is *tell-tale*) is wide board at bottom of front wall. English use board only, still it makes different sound. Americans put strip of tin, this makes a loud buzz when ball hits.

Many times you hit tin in beginning. A good experienced player, he hits tin, he feels like carpenter hitting thumb with hammer.

If you have first chance to hit ball, you are server, you put your foot in service box, throw ball in air and serve. Ball must go to front wall first, higher than service line. It can bounce on other walls after, but it must come down inside service court on other side from you, this is where your opponent waits.

If you play English game, you can make points

only when you are *hand-in*, this is when you are serving. If your opponent keeps making mistakes, you stay *hand-in*, you keep serving. But when *you* make a mistake, now you are *hand-out*, your opponent serves, he is *hand-in*, he has chance to make points. If you get 9 points before opponent, you win game.

In American game, you make a point every time your opponent makes a mistake or you make a winner, it makes no difference who serves ball. You keep service until you do not return ball properly. Same also for opponent. You make 15 points first, you win game.

This is rule enough for a while: now we talk about ball and racquet.

ball

What can one say about ball? You can see it is a small black rubber ball, less than one ounce. Important thing you do not see. Hollow, this ball. When it is cold, it is hard, it sleeps, it does not wish to play. But you knock it up a bit, air in hollow inside warms up and pushes to get out, it becomes like a spring. Now this ball bounds with joy.

English ball is little bit more small than American ball, also more soft. You can push it in easy with your thumb, you hit this ball hard it spreads out on wall, people tell me this is how they think of name for this game, ball going "squash" against wall.

I play with English ball for 30 years, then I come to United States for Open matches in 1954. I have surprise. This American ball wants to leap like a cat. Like a cat it has nine lives. I have to learn how to put it away.

Do not worry, you learn to move with your proper ball.

racquet

Most places where you go to play they give you court and ball, but I think they look for you to buy racquet, yes? Another player does not give his good racquet to use, it is like toothbrush, personal. He thinks it is not same when you give it back after some games. Maybe he is right!

I do not tell you how much to pay, what name on handle, this is not my affair. Also, this is advertising. No, I just show you difference in racquets.

You look at many racquets and you say, *what* difference? They all have small head, 9 inches wide on strings, long thin handle, whole racquet 27 inches. Nice varnish on every one.

But you see difference in court. A good racquet has good wood, it has spring, it is tough. You take this racquet in your hand, it is not too heavy in head, not too light. It has good balance. It lasts to take new strings three or four times, shoulder stays strong, head does not bend over when strings you pull tight.

Yes, you pay more for such a racquet. You have reasons. Other racquets, few dollars less, they do not play and last like this. Also, sometimes they have nylon strings. Nylon is smooth like glass, you try to spin ball, the ball cannot grab these strings, it slips. And nylon does not bend in for ball. Stiff. After while, it tries to bend in, it breaks.

Good racquets use catgut, from sheep insides. Ball you can spin easy on catgut, it is rough. It bends in, it springs out to help ball where it is going.

51

Good racquets use catgut from sheep insides. Ball you can spin easy on catgut, it is rough. It bends in, it springs out to help ball where it is going.

Myself, I take care to use good catgut in my games. In 1945 I break right elbow playing soccer football in Peshawar, it is never so strong as before, so everytime I have important games, I help this elbow every way. In World Championship matches, I string my racquet very tight with best 17-gauge gut, very thin strings with wonderful spring. With these strings I get a little more speed. They do not fool me, when I stroke, that ball goes very close where I say to go. When I am in a bad position, I cannot make a proper stroke with my arm, a little wrist snap and I can make a good reply.

Only for big matches I buy this gut, I cannot afford often, for regular play I use good grade 16-gauge, a little more thick. When I come to United States I still want to keep my elbow safe, I do not use American racquet, it is 2 ounces more heavy, with thick 15-gauge gut. I keep light English racquet and 16-gauge string, and for title matches only I put in best grade. With hard American ball, 17-gauge soon breaks.

I tell you this to show you what racquet does for game. I do not tell you to buy best racquet, best gut. Maybe to begin you buy low-price racquet, get good one later. In beginning, maybe when you aim for ball, you hit wall. A few hits on wall, goodbye that racquet.

Last thing about racquet: choose right size grip. If handle is too big, you cannot snap your wrist properly. If it is too small, you must all time squeeze hard so handle does not turn in your hand. You get tired.

grip

I show you grip on racquet like you are right-hand player. Left-hand player can turn around what I say.

You take racquet in your left hand, hold light in the neck with thumb and next finger. Move out your arm and look at this racquet. If you see strings, turn racquet head, you want to see wood only.

Now put out your right hand like you are to shake hands with this racquet, and grip handle. Thumb goes far around, it is like lock. This grip, the way your hand is on top, looks like way you grip hammer to put in nail. One change: move first finger away from second finger up handle a little bit. Look at picture, you see how much. Let it stay, this finger helps steer racquet.

53

You see end of handle? Best to see only a little come out from your hand—one-half inch, no more.

When I am a boy I hold racquet high on handle, three inches come out after my hand. This is because there is no small child racquet. Long time I hold racquet so, yes, I play 1950 English Open with same grip, I am only player you see like this. This match I win, yes, but what reason? Not grip. When I go back to Pakistan, I try proper grip, with hand low on handle, I see I have more reach, more power, more different shots. Never again I use that boy grip.

Some players they have one grip for forehand, other grip for backhand. In rally, they change back, forth, each time they must look to see if they make change right. Where is this time in fast play? This grip I show you, you never change, it is good two ways, forehand, backhand.

You must keep this grip tight when you stroke, yes, but do not squeeze hard always. You get cramp in hand. Sometimes, you see it is safe, rest racquet neck in left hand, let loose a little your fingers. When ball begins to come to you, your hand is happy to grip tight again.

stroke

Some people are in hurry, they do not want to take trouble with squash stroke, they think, "Why so serious, do I study to hit fly with flyswatter?" They want to hit ball, that is all. So they go in court and hit that ball, and they find ways I never see before. One man I watch, he plays many years now, you think he is on horse with polo mallet, the racquet goes in a big circle, you better give room to him. Another man is fencer, he leaps and sends his arm

54

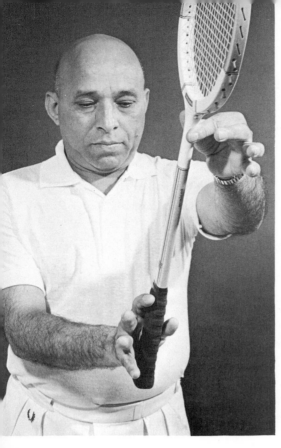

...take racquet in left hand, hold light in neck with thumb and forefinger. Now put out your right hand like you want to shake hands with this racquet and grip handle.

...looks like way you grip hammer. One change: move forefinger up handle about half inch. This finger helps steer racquet.

You see end of handle? Best to see only a little come out from your hand. One half inch, no more.

out like he wants to stab that ball with racquet.

Sometimes these people are good players anyway, but they give themselves handicap. I hope *you* are not in hurry. If you take time to learn proper stroke, then you play better, enjoy more this game.

We pretend you are in right side of court and ball comes to you, low, on right. You want to make a forehand stroke. Here is what you do:

Face right wall, feet wide apart maybe 3-4 inches more wide than shoulders. You can use whole body for power when you face side wall. You face front wall, your arm has no help, it is weak, you try and see. Remember, feet wide apart, you put them close, you fall over when you stroke. Feet wide apart, you have good balance. After stroke, you pick up foot without weight on and can take a big step where you want to go.

Cock wrist, raise it up and swing it back, same direction like when you lift hammer to hit nail. Like this, wrist is strong, it has someplace to go.

Position body, bend the knees a little and a little lean forward and down, from waist. This is *crouch.*

Position arm, put right forearm against upper arm, so right hand comes close to right shoulder. Elbow keep close to body. In fast game better you position your arm like this while you run to get to ball. This way, you are more ready for stroke.

Start backstroke. Bring arm back and up and same time turn body right, left shoulder going down, right shoulder coming up, all turning a little like corkscrew. You know when you reach top of stroke. For everybody, a little difference.

Stroke. You unwind, arm and shoulder coming down, left shoulder starts coming up, forearm uncocks and

FOREHAND
(1) Remember, high backswing is right way to give ball high speed. Small backswing, you chop *at ball:* bad.

(2) Body turning, right shoulder going down, left shoulder going up, eye on ball.

(3) Follow through. Look at racquet: wrist keeps it up, face open. Many players make mistake to close racquet face on hit and follow through.

FOREHAND

(1) Maybe you wonder what you can do with left arm? My idea is put this arm in swing also. Better for balance.

(2) This is proper place to hit ball on forehand—near left knee. See how wrist holds racquet up.

(3) Look at pictures and ever you see how player crouches, bends knees a little, bends body forward from middle.

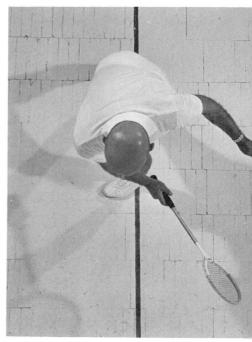

BACKHAND
(1) See how high I make backswing for full power stroke.

(2) Keep feet wide like this for big stroke. Too close, you lose balance.

(3) Careful, you keep wrist high, let not racquet sag down one moment in entire stroke.

BACKHAND

(1) See how upper part your body winds up like spring for backstroke.

(2) Now you let spring go, you unwind.

*(3) I like backhand for reason arm goes **out** from body on stroke, nothing stands in way!*

moves flat at knee high, wrist uncocks and snaps, racquet hits ball a little in front of left knee, weight goes over to left leg, you follow through, and now you pick up right foot and take the big step where you want to go.

Backhand stroke you make like forehand only you face left wall. Everything like before: feet wide apart, crouch a little, cock forearm and wrist, swing arm and body to left, right shoulder going down, left shoulder coming up. Now stroke. Unwind body to right, uncock forearm and swing flat, snap wrist, hit ball a little in front of right knee, follow through, and take big step.

Some players have idea they cannot have good power on backhand, they are weak on this side. Opponents learn this, they put most shots there, they know they get poor reply.

Why is backhand weak! No reason! You look how you stroke! You can see with forehand, arm comes *in* to body at end of stroke, with backhand arm goes *out* from body, nothing stands in way. Yes, body unwinds better on backhand. This stroke should be same for power as forehand, maybe a little more. For me it is so.

power in stroke

Little more talk about wrist. I say put it *high* and *back* for stroke. If wrist hangs down, it is weak, easy to hurt, racquet hangs down, very poor control. High, wrist is strong, you feel your wrist high, it is like arm puts a good brace on it, and high like this it does not snap before right moment. You put wrist *back*, it has more place to go. Impossible to slam a shut door, first necessary you open that door. You open wrist better to snap it.

61

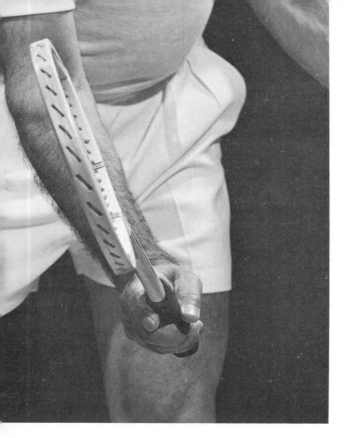

Do something: take position for stroke, hold racquet near front knee, near knee high, where you want to hit ball, and cock your wrist. Now, look at racquet, is it straight up and down to hit ball square? Satisfactory, but you improve this if you turn wrist so racquet strings slant a little back from front wall. This slant makes ball spin back, it hits wall, it wants to get to floor quick and stop bouncing. You learn to stroke very hard with open racquet, you hit front wall just over tin, that ball bounces twice before it comes to service line on floor. You put no spin on this ball, it goes six-seven feet more before second bounce, your opponent returns this easy.

You have a big mirror in your club? Stand in front and watch how you stroke. Watch, correct. Relax, stroke easy. Do not make tense your body, do not try too hard. Swing like you are Tarzan of Apes on some vine. Muscle is not power in squash stroke. Body weight in right place, going right speed, is power.

This low stroke you make in crouch you need to learn right, if you want to play well this game. Only way to get speed on ball when you need it. Some people have difficulty. They know all about knee, wrist, elbow, shoulder, grip, everything, they have difficulty anyway. I know one man, big, arm like blacksmith, good condition, smart, good condition, smart, fast on feet, but you think he has fast on feet, but you think he has fast ball? No! Stiff, this man. Too many tight muscles.

You learn this low stroke, you enjoy feeling very much. It is like you waste nothing, everything goes into that ball when you hit it. I have beginner student, when he strokes ball right, he says he feels like Mickey Mantle hitting home run. Mickey Mantle is American baseball player.

chapter 3

keep eye on ball

1

Ever I see new player who wants to practice stroke in mirror, go in court by self alone to hit ball, this is big surprise for me. Most people, they find out about squash racquets, they look quick for opponent to play game. They have outfit, new rubber shoes, shirt, pants, racquet, they know rules enough. They are ready.

Maybe you are like this? Good luck!

Last chapter in this book I say idea of this game is place ball so opponent does not return it properly. Quite right. But do not worry to make problems for your opponent yet, I think maybe you have plenty problems yourself.

For start I give you some few other things to remember.

keep safe

Not dangerous sport, squash racquets, nobody ever killed in court, I hear about. But you play other beginner like you are, watch out anyway. Keep safe!

Hard to remember. You go in that court, you have one idea: win game. You do not worry about self. You do not stop to see, "Do I face side wall, cock wrist right?" You think you learn right way later, right now you have game to win, and you swing racquet to smash ball so opponent never catches it.

Ball looks like it tries to leave game. You aim front, it goes sideways. It hits lights, ceiling, it flies in gallery. Sometimes you swing, you never make hit and ball keeps going, you look to see are strings in racquet yet.

You do not care, you have joy in this game. But watch out anyway. Keep safe. Give opponent plenty room.

Maybe ball comes close to you, it is opponent's turn to hit, he is beginner, he cannot think about two things same time yet, you better move quick.

With correct stroke, elbow stays pretty close to body, stays bent some on follow-through. Many beginners, they forget this. They do not bend elbow, they put arm out straight for swing, on follow-through racquet comes up high and far out from body. Watch out! Beginner like this is same as helicopter in court. You hear those strings sing in your ear, you are pretty close!

There is a young lawyer who comes to my club, excellent player, state "A" rank. Good sportsman. Beginners ask him for game, he does not look for excuse, he says, "Why not?" One time in court he forgets who he plays and comes too close. When beginner asks him for game now, he says, "Why not?" In locker now he keeps hard white hat like for driver of race car and wire fence for face. Still good sportsman!

get in shape

Do not all the time play beginner, get some games

with good player in your club. He does not ask you. You ask him.

With good player you find out quick how is your condition.

He does not kill the ball to make points. No, he gives you chance every time to hit, he sends ball slow where you are not, still you can run to get it. You are in back, he sends ball up front. You are in front, he sends it over head to back. You are on right side, he sends it left.

That is all right, you are happy in court with good player, you show him you not give up easy. You fight hard to win point. And once in while, he says, "Good get! You were there! Too bad!" such things.

You run like crazy man round court fifteen-twenty minutes, you are all wet, salt water in eyes, chest jumping up and down to get air, legs weak. You drop on floor, put back against wall. Opponent is dry, chest quiet like he just comes in court. He looks at you worried. "You all right?" he says.

You all right, yes. Just not in shape.

Many different ideas how to get in shape for this game: skip rope, lift weights, stretch exercises, run on road one-two miles every day, run upstairs-downstairs, run in one place with feet coming off floor few inches. You want to do such things?

My idea is play squash racquets, best way to get in shape for this game. But maybe you are not so young any more—like me, sometimes little stiff? Then, first loose up your muscles before you play. Do few sit ups, some squats, touch toes, that is all. Soon you are loose, you can go in court.

Some time I see player come out of court early, he is leaning on opponent to walk. Muscle in leg pulled! Now he is out of game 3-4 weeks. I see this man when he goes in court, cold, right away from locker room, but anyway I say, "Too bad! You warm up little?" He says, "Warm up? That good idea?" Yes, good idea!

Any way you do it, it is important you get in shape. How do you stroke properly, move properly, when all time you do not know where you get next breath?

If you are fat man, big tummy, I tell you squash racquets never takes this weight from you. I am in court six-seven hours every day, and never I lose one ounce like this. Eat not so much, only way. When you are too heavy, you do not like to watch food, don't worry, you can play, you learn to be good player. Only you do not last too long in court.

I tell you little story. Year 1951 I play Abdul Bari, top-rank player from Bombay, in English Professional Match finals in London. Abdul Bari has many shots, he can hit ball very hard, then next stroke, send ball to float like cotton puff to front wall just over tin.

This is best drop shot ever I see anywhere. But Abdul Bari is weak one way: not good retriever. This is for reason he is not built like good retriever; he is big man, big chest, shoulders, legs, very heavy for squash player— over 180 pounds and only 5'8" high. He carries 70 pounds I do not carry. I am 112.

I play very fast game, try to keep him off balance, make him turn and run so he does not get set to play those good shots. He runs well, first game. Extra weight does not bother him for while. Second game, I see he begins to go a little more slow, few times he is late to ball. He takes deep, deep breath after rallies. Extra weight makes him begin to work harder and harder. He looks tired.

Outside court after this game, he says, "Hashim,

impossible I run any more like this! We go back, I do not try, you win quick." I look at him: this man is cousin mine, he comes from my village, Nawakille, he does not play for self, he plays for India. I say, "No, it is not right I win three straight, I put ball more close to you so you do not run so far."

I do like I say, I give him ball more in hand and Abdul Bari hits ball well now, and makes delightful drop shots. He wins third game. I send ball to make him run some, so gallery sees some action, but he turns and moves more and more slow. Anyway, he makes enough kills to win fourth game. Now match stands 2-2.

Outside court before last game, Abdul Bari says, "Hashim, finish this game quick." He is very tired. I say, "No, play, make a score, I do not want you to have zero." We go back. First stroke Abdul Bari makes, he hits tin. Mistake? I give him easy service. He hits tin. Again I serve. Tin. Nine times he sends ball to tin. He cannot play.

I am sorry to win like this. It is like Abdul Bari comes on court with sack cement on back. Maybe if this man not so heavy, he shows he is best player.

crouch

From beginning all the time crouch a little when you play.

Some players wait for ball in court like I see people stand around at cocktail party, little drink in hand. Too relaxed. Ball comes to them, they think, "Ah, here comes ball, I get ready." They get ready too late.

Why you think tiger goes to crouch when it waits for dinner in bushes? Better to spring. Same for squash player.

"T"—best place to stay before you know where opponent sends ball. Crouch, keep feet wide, weight forward, ready for big step right, left, front, anywhere.

Crouch. Bend knees a little, feet apart, lean forward a little from middle. Hold racquet up, do not let sag down near floor, hold up, ready across your middle. Now you can quick spring anywhere with big step, play forehand, backhand, you waste no time.

go to "T"

"T," where stripes come together on floor, is best place for you when you wait for turn to hit and you do not know where opponent sends ball. Not every time possible, quite right. Sometime opponent takes this place first. Anyway, ever you can, go there. And one time I know you can go certain: after you serve. After serve, and you do not come in way of opponent (proper he has clear shot where he wants to send ball), go quick to "T."

Close I watch son Sharif to see where he sends ball. Look how he crouches for stroke, how I crouch also. In moment I see he plays low, hard alley shot.

Quick I turn, take giant step to get in position for my stroke. This way I have more time to get set.

When you are here, difficult for opponent to pass you with low fast ball. You have time to go quick right, quick left, for get. If he gives you high shot, overhead, no worry, you have plenty time to reach this ball in back court. If he has idea to give you soft low shot to make ball die up

70

front, you watch this, you run fast as can up front, most times I think you arrive in time for get.

Yes, "T" is very strong place in court!

take big step

When you see where opponent has idea to place ball, take big step in proper direction. If you stand in court right way, face to front wall, in crouch, feet wide, easy to do this. Just you turn body, put one foot in air and move out strong for big, big step. You save time this way, you get in good position quick for your stroke. Best way to move for all players. Even you are high like Jolly Green Giant, take big step!

move quick

Other day in my club, I stand in gallery, watch game with two beginners. One man in left back court, other man opposite. First man hits soft shot up front. Other man, he watches. He sees ball leave racquet slow, go slow to front wall, hit maybe 3 feet over tin, come out slow and bounce one time on floor. He watches very close. All of sudden he moves. He runs very fast up front, swings racquet hard. Too late. Second bounce. He picks up ball and throws it to friend in back. "*That* is good shot," he says. Friend says, "Thank you!"

For while, maybe *you* stand and watch. You cannot help, you have no experience to know how ball behaves.

71

You wait to see where it goes. When it is more quiet, you move.

After few games, you begin to think in front of that ball. You see what speed it leaves racquet, direction, how high, you have good idea where ball goes. But maybe you do not move yet? I understand this. Your reflex does not work good yet.

Some players, they stand and watch ball go, lose point, they get angry at self. They say, "Move, dammit!" some such thing, loud, better to remember next time. They see mistake.

When you know you wait too long, this is good, then you begin to move more quick. Opponent hits ball, you go quick as can to place where you think you make your stroke. Pretty soon, you begin to move when ball is maybe only one second from racquet. Later you move at end of opponent's stroke. Yes, and you become experienced, quick-think player, few years in court, maybe you learn to watch opponent's feet to tell how hard he hits, you watch his wrist, wrist begins to move, you tell direction, you start to move at start of stroke. It is like you read mind.

Long time ago in Peshawar, young man, not good squash player, he swings wild at ball any way he can, wants to go in court with me to see how many points he gets. His friends laugh. They say, "You never make point, Hashim knows where that ball goes before you hit." Young man says, "Impossible! When I hit, I do not know where goes that ball myself!"

take time

Opponent hits, you move quick as can, yes, so you

72

arrive before second bounce. Sometimes you arrive early. Excellent! If you are early, do not rush, take time to make good shot. You come close to proper place and you see you have time, make ready your position, judge for proper distance to ball, not too close, not too far, put feet right for balance. Then make shot.

Difficult lesson. You learn to move quick, you want every moment to move quick. Some experienced players never learn to take time, they are very fast on feet to ball, but they hurry stroke, off balance, too near, too far, no difference, they stroke. They make bad shot.

Try to remember: move quick as can to gain time. Then take care with stroke. You learn this, you do a very good thing for your game.

Not always you have time, I know this. Maybe you run fast as can, then you do splits like dancer to reach that ball. You cannot stroke, you cannot snap wrist properly. You are happy so that ball goes anywhere on front wall.

Sometimes, it is no difference how you try, you see you are too far from ball. What do you do? I tell you idea I have what to do. This happens in Toronto in finals, Canadian Open matches, 1963, and I am in court with Henry Salaun, very fine American player.

In one game, Mr. Salaun makes wonderful drop shot, I rush fast to front and make weak return. Now I am in bad position, near front wall, in middle. Mr. Salaun, in bad position also, makes soft shot near left corner. I see I cannot reach ball, no time to take step, so I take quick aim and send racquet from my hand. Racquet hits ball after first bounce, ball goes up and hits wall over tin. Gallery laughs. I laugh. Mr. Salaun laughs also, but he calls, "Let!" because I am in way of him. We play point over.

73

I play this shot 3 times in 25 years of matches. Enough.

keep eye on ball

Cat never takes eye from bird it tries to catch and never you take eye away from ball you want to hit. *Keep eye on ball* is most important one thing I tell you about this game of squash racquets.

Yes, you decide where you send ball. You look to see where opponent is, you look quick to see where you send that ball, before you stroke. Now, no more look. You have picture of court in your head. It does not change, walls do not move. But ball you cannot keep in head, it moves, you need to watch.

Some time beginner keeps eye on ball for while. Then, start of stroke, he takes eye away to look up. He is interested to see where goes ball when he hits it, he is not sure what happens. He like it to go one way, but he thinks maybe it goes other.

Do not look up. Watch ball in stroke. Eye is wonderful quick to follow that ball, to tell body, "One moment please! A little closer! Snap wrist now!" such things, so ball goes to center of strings and flies out to proper place in court.

You look in your club where members hang racquets. You do not need to look for names on handles, you tell good players by strings: catgut wears most in center, rest of strings most like new and no ball marks on frame. Eye puts ball in center.

Many beginners take eye away from ball for reason they think they cannot see what happens anyway, too

Keep eye on ball...is most important one thing I tell you.

fast, so they look at something else they are sure they see.

Not easy in beginning, I know this. But try. Even you think you do not see, watch. Eye faster than you think. Later on, you catch up with self, you can see what eye sees.

Keep eye on ball!

chapter 4

Ground Stroke and Volley

4

This chapter we talk about two kinds squash stroke — one you make *after* bounce, that is ground stroke, one you make *before* bounce, that is volley.

ground stroke

I tell you some about ground stroke in other chapter: position for racquet, hand, wrist, forearm, elbow, feet, trunk, your body, shoulder, and how you swing body to hit ball. Yes, lot to remember. You practice by self in mirror, soon you do everything right, but you go in court with opponent, maybe memory is upset? Like waiter, he carries tray with big stack dishes, nobody in way, he is all right, but he goes into other waiter coming out of swing door, there goes those dishes.

Maybe you play enough games now so you are not upset, you remember better, I hope. I like to put few more dishes on your tray.

Best place for ball? Where do you like ball for best ground stroke? High as knee is where. Best for control, best for power. Body hangs right to stroke ball high as knee, every man is same.

Not always you have chance like this. Sometime

ball is low like ankle, soon it is dead, you bend down more, you stroke best you can anyway. Sometime ball is high. Again you stroke. But you have ball, after bounce, higher than waist, better I think you wait for bounce from back wall. Body not built to make proper ground stroke so high.

Speed you send ball. You have good control of speed if you use body right, understand how parts work. Wonderful system for stroke: trunk of your body, upper arm, forearm, wrist. They move 1, 2, 3, 4, each one little more fast. Number 4, that is wrist, goes most fast for reason it has speed of others, then puts own speed on top. 4 is like booster for 1, 2, 3.

When you want very fast ball, you make full back stroke, use more muscle to unwind trunk of your body fast, send arm through fast, snap wrist like flash, then you have top speed on racquet moment it hits that ball. Some player, they try this, they remember 1, 2, 3, they forget 4. Maybe they are big men, strong body — no difference, they do not hit hard ball. Remember: wrist swings racquet, speed of ball is how fast that racquet swings.

You want slow ball, you take same position, make stroke same way, but everything — 1, 2, 3, 4 — is more slow.

You are in forecourt, you want very soft ball, take right position, no back swing, make baby stroke with forearm, turn wrist easy, make little follow through.

Many new player, they are afraid they hit ball too hard, they forget position, they reach out arm and *poke* ball with racquet. Ball does not know where to go. I appreciate you do not do this.

You are beginner, do not worry to get top speed on ball. You try too hard, you begin to chop at ball, tighten up muscles. Your body learns good motion, good timing for medium-pace ball, then it tells you when ready to give more speed. Do not hurry self.

Direction you send ball. Other chapter, when I tell about ground stroke, I say hit ball when it comes close to knee — left knee for forehand stroke, right knee for backhand stroke. When it comes to front knee, face of racquet is straight — it goes same way like front wall. And ball goes out from racquet straight. Like this you make alley shot I tell you about later.

But you want ball to go cross-court, make little change. Lean in little, direction of side wall, let elbow out little more from body, and hit ball few inches *before* it comes to front knee. Now racquet is not straight with front wall, it has angle, and ball goes out cross-court like you want. Reason for little change in body and elbow is so center of strings meet ball.

For reason racquet has angle, not square to ball, I personal give little more snap to wrist on cross-court shot. Also for reason I lean in little more, I have more wrap-round follow through.

Do not change feet. Face side wall like for alley shot. Some player, they want to cross ball, they put front foot behind other, they aim body way they want ball to go. They have bad stroke. Also, opponent looks at feet, he knows which way ball goes before hit.

Experienced player I know, he leans back from waist to make this cross-court shot. Yes, ball crosses over, for reason he does right thing, hits ball early. He leans back anyway, like he helps *pull* that ball over. Nervous habit.

Stroke from back wall. Like I say before, ball more high than waist is bad for ground stroke. Many times, ball

78

has good speed, you hurry, you can get it off back wall. Some players do not go all way to back wall. They just move little way. They think, "Why run? Ball comes back to me in one moment." Sometimes fooled, these lazy players! Ball bounces only little. Emergency. They quick have to reach *behind* and hook that ball to send it up front. Bad stroke!

Much better you run to back wall and — you have time — take position: face side wall, one foot close to back wall crack, other foot put out wide to front, make stroke and hit ball when it comes out to front knee. For forehand, backhand, same. You stand like this, even ball comes out weak, you have racquet *behind* it, you have good control.

Some student, I show them to put foot near crack, they think they have no room for back swing, afraid they crash racquet to back wall. Yes, true, they crash racquet

When you take ball from back-wall, better you go close to crack. Even when ball comes out weak, you have racquet behind *it, you have good control.*

all right for reason swing is too much *back*, not enough *up*.

Next time in court, try idea. Put foot near crack. How far from wall to front knee — 24 inches anyway, yes? Enough room for curve-down, flatten-out stroke with wrist snap on end? Yes, when your racquet hits back wall, better change back stroke.

Back on ball. Sometime opponent gives you big 3-wall shot — ball goes to front-wall, to side-wall, to back-wall, *then* bounces first time to floor in back court. Maybe he gives you such shot on service, well, you need to say thanks to him. He gives you set-up!

If you stand in right court and opponent kindly gives you such a ball, coming on your right, do like this. Keep face to this ball, move backwards so not to let ball go behind you. Keep eye on ball on side wall, back wall, judge where it bounces on floor, back away to this place. Ever keep eye on ball! At same time take crouch, start back swing, corner of eye tells you is court clear for ball to travel. At proper moment you stroke on forehand.

When you stand in left court and you get this same 3-wall shot on your left side, back away from ball like before, only this time you make stroke on *backhand*.

Now in left court, some players do not like to back on ball. They like to turn body round, so when ball bounces on floor they have position to take stroke on *forehand*.

Player with idea to go round like this supposed to say "Turning!" or "Round," loud. It is like man saws big tree in woods, tree begins to fall, he says "Timber!" for reason he cannot control this tree, everybody better run out of way. Squash player says "Turning!" for reason he cannot see where is his opponent when he goes round, he thinks maybe he cannot control not to hit this man when he strokes, opponent better run out of way. Opponent, he is smart, makes self very small, gives player whole court for shot. Fast squash ball stings worse than bee.

My personal game, always I back on ball when I am lucky to have opponent give me this 3-wall shot. Never I turn. I back on ball, corner of eye tells me every moment is court clear, what shot I can make. If I *turn* on ball, I am blind for moment, I wonder, "Where is opponent?"

My idea is turning on ball is bad sports, also bad for control. Better I think you always *back* on ball.

Change mistakes. Not many times I see new player learn easy and quick to make good ground stroke in game. Most new player have trouble. You make mistakes, do not worry, you are human, just try to change soon. For while your game is like soft cement, you push around easy, then it becomes stiff, later you want to change something, you need dynamite.

New player, all he keeps in head for while is run and put racquet where ball is. He has no room to think to fit body to ball. Ball maybe too close, too far, too high, too much in front, behind, no different, he hits. He thinks maybe something is wrong, but he does not know what. He hits.

After while, he plays maybe 100 games, he has room in head to think more what he does with body. Now is time to change mistakes. Some player never make change. They play, play, play, they become pretty good even they move wrong, stroke wrong, think wrong. But after while, these mistakes cannot let them play better. One time in London theatre I see man play piano with mittens on hands. He plays not bad with mittens. Also, not very good.

Yes, you are beginner, soon as can, start to watch self — how you move in court, how you stroke. Do not be sorry you lose game for reason you take care. Let opponent be happy he wins. You can be happy you make some few good strokes.

Watch. Change. You let ball come too close, can't stroke with racquet near stomach? Next time, judge ball early, move body to proper position. You stroke right, but no power? Maybe you hit ball little late. Try little earlier, in front of front knee. You hit tin all time? Maybe wrist is not cocked. Check. Also check to see if you have proper position . . . crouch — feet apart — face side wall!

Yes, true, maybe you lose many games ever checking, checking, checking. But this way you correct mistakes, you learn to move and stroke properly. And after while, you have room in head to think how to beat opponent!

volley

Ground stroke is bread-butter stroke for squash game, but you have chance, good you put some little jam on top, play volley.

Volley is when you take ball in air before bounce on floor.

For volley, forehand, backhand, no difference, you face side wall, wrist cocked, arm cocked, you make full stroke, with wrist snap and follow through.

You can play low volley, ball low as knee, maybe little more low, but watch you do not sag your racquet. Bend self down low, keep racquet more high than wrist.

You can volley high, but there is limit. Not so high you need to put arm out straight over head to reach ball. High so you still have good crook in arm, then you can stroke properly.

With volley, you can smash ball hard, play light

like feather, send ball straight, cross court, to corner, anywhere.

Volley steals time from opponent. He makes his stroke, he likes to go to good position, get set, watch to see what you do. If you run to catch that ball after bounce, maybe he has 2-3 seconds. Nice for him. But you move quick to volley, you think quick where to put that ball, opponent has shock. You steal his time. He does not worry what he does to you, he worries does he reach ball before second bounce. You put pressure on him.

stop volley

If opponent gives you very hard ball pretty high, high like shoulder anyway, good idea sometime you play stop volley. You play properly, maybe it is stop rally also. You quick put racquet up, firm grip on handle, tilt face where you want ball to go. Never you stroke, just hold still that racquet. Into strings, ball goes like lion, comes out like lamb, goes soft to front wall, dies quick. You get free ride on opponent's muscle.

half volley

Half volley, you hit small moment after bounce on floor. You do not see bounce for reason racquet is in way to make stroke, you learn proper timing by trying many times. You are wrong by one hair, you spoil this shot.

Half volley you can play close to body. You do not crouch and this time, quite proper, racquet head droops down, you make easy little stroke in front of body. Some-

83

For volley, face side wall, wrist cocked, arm cocked, make full stroke. When necessary you stretch arm straight to reach, then that ball is too high for good stroke, better you catch on bounce from back wall.

Half-volley you can play close to body. This time, quite proper, racquet head droops down. You hit ball small moment after bounce.

time I see chance, I am in forecourt, opponent more back, he hits medium-fast ball, I play half-volley drop. Opponent has trouble to arrive in time.

But if you play half-volley away from body and go to crouch, you need to keep racquet up over wrist. Sometime when you are in middle court, opponent in back, he tries to pass you with fast cross-court shot. Maybe you can quick reach out away from body, catch that ball on half-volley, play soft to front.

volley is think stroke

Volley is more difficult than ground stroke for reason you must think more quick. If you are beginner, you are maybe quick to hit, you do not think where is best place to put shot. You are happy to meet ball in air, that is all.

Sometime I see two player in rally, they stand mid-court, one right side, one left side, they volley back, forth, back, forth, they are like boxers who do not think to box, they put toes to toes, punch, punch, punch body of other. Then mistake occurs. One player hits with wood of racquet, ball goes out of bounds. Other player says, "Good rally."

Yes, good rally. Good practice for eye to take ball in air. But remember: volley is think stroke like ground stroke. Soon as can, begin to think where to put ball, what speed.

chapter 5

Service

service is very important

Some squash players, plenty of experience and no excuse, have wrong idea about serve. They think it is not important, just signal to begin, like bell in boxing match. Not so! Service in squash racquets is not like bell. It is like first punch . . . maybe K.O.!

One player with wrong idea like this, when he puts foot in box never he has idea in head of best place to send ball to opponent. Not interested, this man. Better he likes the game *after* serve. Run fast, jump, twist, volley, slug ball hard as can, this is game he likes. Wham. Pow.

Many games he loses. He knows reason and this reason he does not like. He goes out from court with opponent, he says, "You win on serve, many points you make like that." Like score is not fair. Opponent, he feels very good for reason he wins, he wants to give compliment to loser, he says, "Yes, take away my serve, maybe *you* win. You are tiger in rally." Loser likes to hear this, he likes to have name of tiger. He says to himself, private: "I learn to handle this man's serve, you wait, I chew him up in court!"

Yes, good idea he learns to handle opponent's serve, but why he does not think to learn good serve himself?

You want to be like tiger in rally, all right, just be

86

smart tiger. You put foot in box, think what you do and do best you can.

You have serve, you have advantage. You have rule to watch, yes, you must hit ball to front wall over service line, send ball so it goes to bounce in service court where opponent waits. No difference, still you have advantage anyway. You have chance to put ball so opponent makes weak return and—you are not in way of his shot—you have first chance to go to good center position in court, "T."

Every time you serve, you start strong, you have chance to get more strong, opponent has difficulty not to get more weak. Maybe rally is like this: (1) Good serve, (2) Weak reply, (3) Good shot, (4) Very weak reply, (5) Very good shot! Maybe number 6 shot never you see for reason opponent cannot handle number 5. Very good, you take this point. But watch out: if you make *bad* serve at start, opponent has chance for strong reply, *he* has best chance to win rally!

Now I tell you about some few good serves: lob, slice, hard serve.

lob serve

For good lob, you need ceiling 18 feet high anyway. You are in court with low ceiling, only couple feet over "Out" line on front wall, impossible to make proper lob, maybe you better try other kind of service.

I tell you about lob like you have satisfactory ceiling.

When you are right-hand player, and serve from right court, do not face side wall square to hit ball. Turn little to front. It is like you draw straight line between feet, this line has same direction like ball when it goes to front wall. You put feet like this, you help aim.

Two ways to stroke. Some player like to drop racquet head low near floor, swing up to hit ball near knee-high, little in front of body. Other player like to serve from side, hit ball more high, near shoulder. This way I like.

Swing body to make smooth your stroke, start weight on right foot. Lob is nice, soft stroke.

Here is what you like ball to do. It goes high to front wall, left side, it hits place maybe 6 feet from side wall, 4 feet under top line. It goes back from front wall, higher, higher, like back of cat seeing dog. In back court it goes down.

Almost straight it goes down, like somebody drops this ball from ceiling. It hits side wall soft, little under side line, bounces on floor in service court, near back

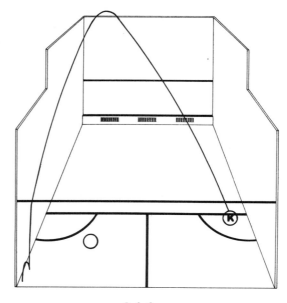

Lob Serve

88

wall. After bounce, this ball wants to go back some more, yes, but more it wants to go *sideways,* for reason it hits side wall going pretty near straight down. So now it touches back wall after bounce, it comes out only a little. More it goes sideways. Quick it dies.

You are receiver, what do you do? You try to play this ball after it hits back wall, it is like you try to get egg off fry pan with your squash racquet. You are top-rank player, wrist like strong steel spring, still I do not think you return this ball after bounce from back wall.

This is perfect lob.

From left court, you serve lob same way, but more difficult to make perfect when you are right-hand player. Ball goes from racquet more close to opponent's side wall. Goes high same way, goes down same way, but hit on side wall is little different. After bounce on floor, this ball wants to go more to back, not so much sideways. A little more it comes off back wall after bounce. *Opponent has better chance to return.*

Never player lives to serve perfect lob every time. If you can do this, you be like machine I see one time, push button, clay plate flies out from trap for people to shoot with gun. Plate goes same way, exact, every time for reason *machine* sends it.

You are not machine. Every time, there is little difference the way you send that ball.

Little difference is all right. Maybe lob is not perfect, but good serve anyway. But you go too far away from right journey of ball, you have trouble.

Maybe ball hits side wall too early, not close enough to back wall. This ball does not push opponent back in corner. He volleys that ball off side wall and makes good shot.

Or maybe you send ball so it does not go to side

wall anywhere, it goes high to back wall only. Easy to return.

Or maybe you serve too strong: ball goes too far back, hits side wall, back wall, bounces, and comes out in service court. Too bad for you, this happens. Opponent goes to play this ball, near center court. Necessary you stay out of way to give him clear shot, this is rule, you stay in back near side wall. He takes time, puts ball away very soft up front, I think you never get there in time!

slice serve

What is idea of slice serve? Make ball fly fast back from front wall, go to hit very low on side wall, little

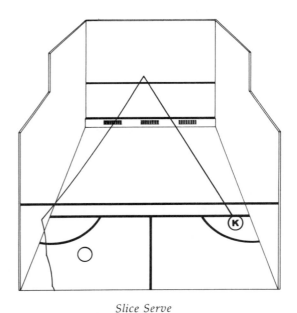

Slice Serve

behind opponent's floor service line, bounce low to back wall.

You serve from right, place ball just little over service line on front wall, and little *left* from center. You serve from left, one change: place ball little *right* from center of front wall.

One thing I wait to tell you about slice, maybe most important thing. You give ball *spin, high-speed back spin.*

After ball hits front wall, it wants to spring back, yes, of course. Also, same time, it wants to *sit down* quick. This not accident, this is purpose of high-speed back spin. You *want* ball to come down quick, so it hits side wall *low,* close to floor.

You think front wall takes all spin from this ball? You have slow, weak spin, yes, maybe true. But when you have good strong high-speed spin, no, not true. Plenty spin left. Ball spins on first bounce to floor. Spin makes ball try to bounce quick again before it goes to back wall.

You put spin on ball and it hits something, wall, floor, it springs away more fast than regular bounce. It *jumps,* this ball, like it has life its own. Ball behaving in such manner, more difficult for opponent to handle.

Slice I tell you about is *side* stroke, you cannot make properly overhead. From *side* you serve. Put elbow out from body, forearm cocked halfway, open up face of racquet, make hard, fast *side* stroke, high as shoulder. Last moment, before hit, snap wrist for more speed.

You are ready to serve, wait one second. Think careful what you try to do, this way you learn more quick to make correct stroke. You try to get fast back spin. If you keep this in head, you see strings must go *under* ball, ball must *roll* on strings. You see reason for stroke from

91

side, reason for open face of racquet: you want strings *under* ball, ball must roll.

Not easy to spin fast, this squash ball. Tennis ball different — big, light, fuzz outside like hair on carpet, you spin this ball very easy. Squash ball small, smooth, hard — more difficult.

Remember, stroke very fast. Ball goes out from racquet not so fast, for reason face is open, you do not hit square. You give away some speed on ball, you get some spin.

You serve proper slice, this ball goes fast and low to side wall, close to floor service line, I do not think your opponent tries volley. If bad serve, ball too high, too far from side wall, yes, he volleys, maybe he puts ball away. But low spin ball, close to side wall, difficult to volley.

Better for opponent, he waits. Maybe he plays after first bounce. If good slice serve, this not easy: ball jumps fast, low to floor. Maybe opponent backs in front of ball, has idea he catches it off back wall. But he must move very quick, no time to get set, I do not think he puts ball away. Maybe he plays cross-court shot in corner. Most times, not perfect, this return, you run fast you have time to make get and hit strong shot.

Slice, even not perfect, is good serve for reason ball chases opponent. Most times, he does not volley: he cannot control this shot. So he must run backwards away from this low fast ball to place where it begins to go slow. But he has no time for careful aim. Slice, good slice, puts pressure on opponent.

Difficult to make good slice. For while you try this serve, you have all kinds trouble: not enough spin, ball too high on front wall, too high and too far back on side wall, bounces too high from floor, too high from back wall. For opponent, just right; for you bad luck. Maybe you better take time, practice in court alone for while. For reason it is difficult, do not give up. For reason it is difficult, not many players learn right. *You* learn, maybe you make some points like this.

hard serve

You make hard serve, you send ball to fly like it goes out from cannon so opponent does not think fast enough what to do for good return. High speed is idea.

You are in right court, left court, no difference, take

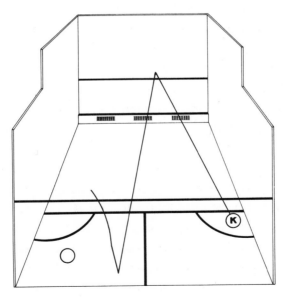

Hard Serve—To Opponent

position halfway face to right side wall, halfway to front wall, same like for lob service. Cock wrist. Now lean back like American big league pitcher to throw fast ball. Bring racquet back over right shoulder. Toss ball in air with left hand and now stroke through fast, overhand. Before you hit ball, snap wrist for more speed on racquet. Hit ball flat.

Where do you send this fast ball? I tell you three places.

To opponent. What you try to do is send ball to bounce from front wall to back wall, hit floor in opponent's court near middle-service line. When ball goes low on back wall *before* bounce on floor it comes fast out in court. But you hit floor *first*, ball comes out slow, it is like you give present to opponent. You hit back wall and floor *same time,* this is crack, ball *rolls out,* you have ace. This is luck, nobody aims so good. So better you not put idea of crack in your head. Try for hit low on back wall and stroke.

You are over six feet high, strong arm, not necessary you serve high on front wall. Little man needs to serve higher, maybe two feet higher than service line.

When you serve from right court, aim for spot on front wall little *right* from center. You serve from left, aim to hit little *left* of center.

This serve is like cowboy quick draw. You put foot in box, you take time, you relaxed, opponent thinks maybe you give him soft serve. All of sudden, you wind up, stroke fast, you fire that ball right at him. What does he do? Maybe he quick puts up racquet like reflex and makes weak reply: then you have advantage. Or he jumps away, he turns to catch ball on return from back wall: ball bounces high enough, he makes good return, now *he* has advantage. Or maybe you surprise him hundred percent. Not one muscle he moves. It is like he does not see what happens. Ball cannot help, it hits him. Looks funny, this hit, you like to laugh. But wait one moment: does opponent think such hit is funny? Be polite, let opponent laugh first!

This serve is gamble. When you do not hit opponent, do not hit crack in back, watch out. Now opponent has center court for return. You are in corner. Maybe curtains for you?

To opponent's corner. This is high-speed cross-court ball. When you serve from right, hit front wall little *left* of center; you serve from left, hit front wall little *right* from center. You want ball to go low on back wall *before* bounce, close to opponent's corner. If you serve right, ball hits back wall, bounces low on floor, goes to side

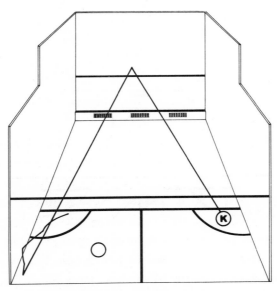

Hard Serve — To Opponent's Corner

95

wall: I do not think opponent makes strong return.

Do not hit ball on front wall too far from center. You make such mistake, ball goes first to side wall in opponent's court, then back wall, then it comes out in center court. Easy for him to put this ball away.

Not difficult for quick opponent, this serve. He is in good position to put racquet up and volley. Maybe he sends that ball low to front wall, near his side wall. Then you have trouble to get to ball in time.

If you try this serve, hit very hard, right direction, everything correct, and still opponent makes good volley return, ask self question: Opponent lucky? Little later, try again. If he volleys good this time, I think maybe you better forget such serve.

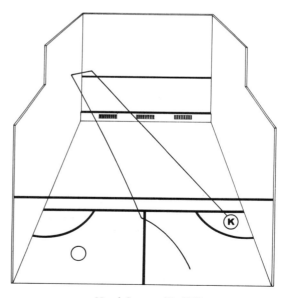

Hard Serve—To "T"

To "T." Hit flat and hard to send ball to front wall little over service line, very close to opponent's side wall. Ball jumps quick to side wall, it flies in front of opponent, it goes down to bounce in his service court near T, now it leaps in *your* service court and hits back wall.

Not easy for opponent to make good return. Ball that comes cross court like so, difficult to judge. Also he must turn body quick, get racquet up, no time to take care.

Experienced opponent, when he sees this ball on way, and he is pretty sure you send it wrong, he does not play this ball, he lets ball bounce out of court, he waits for next serve. But when he thinks maybe your serve is good, he does not wait for bounce, he volleys that ball. Best chance for him.

Why he does not wait for bounce? Well, when he waits for that bounce, he has very hard time to catch that ball. Moves very fast. Also, very important, there is very fast side spin for reason it hits side wall hard very close to corner. Better he play such ball in air. He waits for bounce from floor, from back wall, he does not know how jumps this ball.

Very nice serve, yes. But not easy to make. You send ball just little wrong, it does not go to bounce in corner of opponent's court. Small place you aim for. He has good eye, opponent does not worry, he lets ball go to bounce out of court. One fault for you. Now you have to make safe serve.

more talk about serve

Make difficulty for opponent to return ball: this is

idea of serve. Even he knows what you do before you stroke, some serve difficult for him. Good lob like that. Other serve difficult for reason you surprise him.

You send him lob, lob, lob, lob, some opponent begins to think you are broken record, play same thing all time, he sees you put foot in box, he says to self, "Here comes another lob." Then you give him cannonball serve straight back, I think maybe his brain not believe his eye. He sees ball, yes, he can do nothing in time. Ball hits him. Your point.

You do not surprise good, experienced player easy. He is same as tom cat, he remembers bites he gets in fights, he watches close all round all time. Only time you surprise him, he runs too much, tired, brain goes slow. Then maybe you have chance.

Most times, you see good old player, he serves better than good young player. For reason more experience? No, for reason old player has old legs, they begin to go like rubber when he runs long time. He serves best he can, he looks for short rally, tries to make point quick. Young player, his legs go, go, go, he has joy in long rally, never tired, he is not interested too much in serve.

Man at my club, student mine, more than 55 years old anyway, has good serve I tell you about. He is in right court, he leans out to center, serves lob on backhand. He is in left court, he leans out, serves same way, forehand. Ball goes into opponent's court high, close to side wall, goes closer, closer, bounces in corner.

Always he is very careful, no hurry, he tries to send ball same place every time. Some good young players, he gives them this serve, they have trouble to make strong return, he moves quick, tries to put away that ball with his second stroke. Many points he makes like this. And legs not tired.

Some player like hard serve. Don Legatt like that: he is excellent Canadian amateur, big strong man, not old yet. He sends that ball more fast than ever I see, he serves 100 times, never it goes slow. Some opponents, they go in court with him first time, they have trouble to see the ball, brain does not catch up to tell them what to do. Some other player, they are in match with him before, still they are nervous. Yes, good serve for Mr. Don Legatt!

For my game, in serious match, I use lob and slice, very little hard serve.

I give advice. You are beginner, learn lob. Not easy, ball goes many wrong places for while. Never mind: continue. This is best serve. Learn hard serve next. Slice you learn last: yes, you learn to hit flat first, then later you learn to make spin.

chapter 6

Four Good Shots

6

We talk shots in this chapter — all different shots you need for good game.

First time you go in gallery, watch two excellent players in hard match, you never think to see so many tricks with ball, your eye has trouble to follow what happens, so quick it goes. You get idea these players have hundred different shots, maybe more!

Surprise: these players have *four* shots only, four different shots is total in squash racquets. Total for Mohibullah, Azam, me, professional, amateur, anybody.

Four shots only, but possible to play such shots many different ways. Like *robota*, music instrument in my country. *Robota* has four strings only, but how many sounds come from every string? Same for squash racquets.

Four shots are *alley shot, cross-court shot, drop shot, angle shot.*

alley shot

Alley is little road that runs close all along building. Alley shot is like that. It runs close all along side of court.

Idea is to make difficulty for opponent, of course. You give him ball close to side wall, this is not easy to kill. You make side wall your friend.

Watch you do not hit side wall. You hit side wall, ball comes out in court with air all around, this ball you give to opponent like gift.

Think where you are, then place ball properly. when you stand yourself in alley, hit front wall close to corner. This is true alley shot: ball stays close to side wall every moment. But when you stand more out in court, ball must hit front wall more out from corner. When it goes back, it comes closer, closer to side wall. Still it does not hit.

Yes, good alley shot makes difficulty for opponent. He cannot kill ball. But most times, he can make shot like you also. Yes, with alley shots you see repeats. In many matches I play, maybe six-seven strokes in row are good alley shots. Then there is small mistake: ball comes back

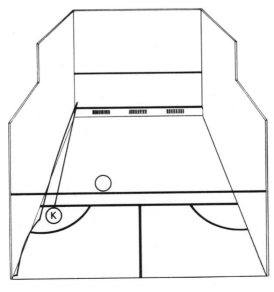

Alley Shot

with some free air around it, enough to play different shot, and one player tries for winner.

Once in while, you can make alley shot opponent does not return. Maybe he gives you bad serve: he tries for lob, but ball comes to you, not too high, and out from side wall. You make overhead smash, hit front wall 2-3 inches over tin, close to side wall. Ball bounces to floor very soon, bounces second time close to service line. Even if your opponent springs fast as can to make return, I think he is late to ball.

When opponent is in "T" and you are in back court, close to side wall, do you play alley shot? Yes, certain kind of alley shot. But not low, soft alley shot. Also not low and hard. Better you play *lob* in alley. Send ball high to front wall, so it comes back for bounce close to back wall. Now you change places: opponent goes to back, and *you* go to "T." What does he do? Same, perhaps: alley lob. If his shot is good, you change places again.

But now maybe he makes small mistake. Maybe ball is not high enough, and comes out, six-seven inches from wall. Now you do *not* go back. You meet that ball near service line, you reach up for over-hand feather stroke and send ball easy and low to front wall, close to side wall. This is favorite shot for me. Many times opponent thinks I have not stretch enough to reach his lob, even bad lob. Yes! I am short man, 5'4". But, he forgets one can leap.

Sometime there is rally in alley, midcourt. You hit hard, low drive, close to side wall, move out quick to let opponent in. He makes same shot. What do you do? High-speed ball close to wall is hot potato, best you send it back quick. I do not think you can make good lob: no time to take care with such shot. Yes, best you make low, hard drive, close to side wall. When you make this shot very

very close, maybe two inches from wall, maybe opponent cannot make high-speed return. Then you run fast to front to catch his slow ball and try for winner.

cross-court shot

Stand on one side of court and send ball to other side: this is cross-court shot. Ball can go high, go low, very fast, quite slow, no difference: when it crosses court, it is cross-court shot!

Take care, this is more gamble than alley shot. When you send ball deep in court, plenty of air around it, necessary you choose right time to place ball so.

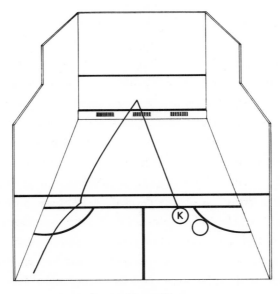

Cross Court Drive

When you stand in back court, near side, and opponent is in "T," is cross-court good shot? No, very bad shot, most times. Opponent twists head round to watch what you do, he keeps body facing front, he is ready to run right, run left. Even you send ball like bullet cross-court, hit front wall two inches over tin, it takes long jump after bounce. If he has not wooden leg, opponent has easy get. *High* cross-court? No. Opponent takes one step and strokes that ball on volley. Cross-court lob? Perhaps. Best you play cross-court lob when opponent is close to front, then you can easy put ball over his head!

Once in while, when opponent in front, cross-court drive is not bad idea. Maybe you make two-three alley

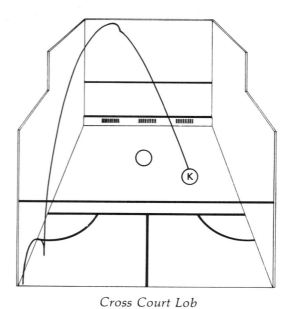

Cross Court Lob

104

shots before. Now opponent gives you soft ball in back of court, out few inches from wall. Opponent twists neck to watch you. You watch him also from corner your eye. You let ball go low before you stroke. Now maybe opponent thinks, "Ah, alley shot again," and he cannot wait one moment more. He takes one foot from floor and begins to move body to face side wall. Now you give him, not alley shot, you give him hard, low cross-court! You pass him with ball for reason he faces wrong way!

Cross-court is good shot when *you* are in front, opponent close behind, little on one side. He stays close for reason he thinks perhaps you play soft, low shot, then he does not have far to run, he will catch that soft ball in time. Now is good time to play hard, low cross-court shot away from him. Open racquet face little more for this shot to give good back spin, and I think this ball bounces twice before it arrives to back wall. High speed is important. If ball is slow, opponent can reach after first bounce. Even you hit that ball too high, high speed passes opponent. He must run to back corner for get.

Sometime when you are in mid-court, near side wall, ready for stroke, opponent comes to mid-court also, he stands by your side. He is fast man perhaps. He thinks you go to play soft drop shot, or low alley shot on your side. He is ready to run. Best play, I think, is hard alley shot on your side, maybe three feet over tin, to make him run to back corner. But once in while for big surprise, you give him cross-court to other side wall! Yes, you hit hard and high that ball. It goes over service line on front wall, it jumps to his side wall, little behind him. Yes, *possible* he gets this ball on volley from front wall. Best for him. But if he thinks too slow for volley, then he must run very, very fast to catch that ball before second bounce.

drop shot

Drop shot is slow ball, it hits just little over tin on front wall, ends quick. It ends more quick if you send it close to corner, so it goes to side wall after front. Side wall is like brake. Yes, and you are lucky, maybe that ball goes to crack at bottom of side wall. When you make drop that hits side wall nick like this, you have very nice shot indeed.

Not too easy to send ball soft to right place. You stroke too hard, ball comes out too far in court. Too soft, maybe you hit tin.

Necessary you make proper stroke. Do not poke that ball. Make a nice stroke, wrist cocked, little backswing, little twist of wrist, racquet open a little, and follow through smooth.

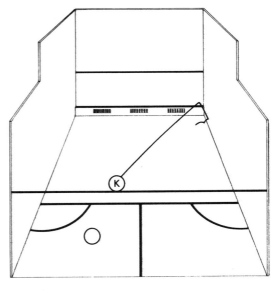

Drop Shot

106

If you are in hurry, play other shot — play angle, alley, cross-court. But you have some chance to get set, then maybe it is good idea to play drop.

Many good player like to put lots of cut on ball for drop shot, they chop down with racquet to rub ball on many strings, give it fast spin. They say ball ends more quick up front. All right for them. Myself, I do not care for this, for reason I lose some control. I use regular stroke, put slow, regular spin on ball, I hit just a little over tin, most times near corner. That ball ends quick enough, I think.

When I come to United States, 1954, never I see drop shot. Americans play alley, cross-court, angle. They play deep in court. So I play drop in match, they are surprised, and I make some easy points. Then they begin watching more close, they practice. They start to make such shots also.

Drop shot is best in cold court: ball does not want to bounce, dies quick in front. In 1963, I play Al Chassard, excellent top professional and fine sports gentleman, in Canadian Open final in Toronto. Very cold February day outside. Very cold February day inside. People in gallery keep heavy coats on. My drop shot works good in such cold, so I play drop, drop, drop, in corners. Mr. Chassard is fast man on feet, he tries, but not enough time. That ball bounces like stone.

angle shot

For angle shot, you send ball to side wall first. Good angle shot goes low to front wall from side wall. Also angle it makes with front wall, is small. This keeps ball close to front wall after bounce, makes opponent run more far.

107

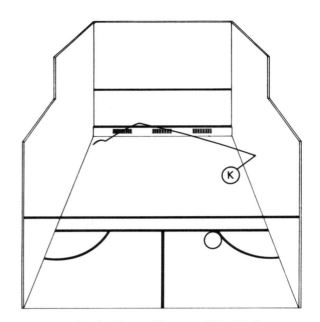

Angle Shot—Close to Side Wall

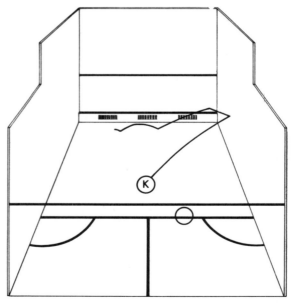

Angle Shot—From Mid Court

For proper angle, watch where to place ball. If you stand close to side wall, hit side wall back far from front corner. If you are out more in court, hit more close to corner. Idea is to keep ball close to front after bounce. You want to hit front wall with small angle.

Angle shot is more easy than drop, for reason you need some speed on ball, you do not try for feather touch.

Like all other shot, necessary you think *when* to play angle. When opponent is behind you, yes, play, if you like. Also, *play to side wall near him.* This way you make sure ball pushes away most far from him, when it goes to front wall.

Sometime, you have experience, you can play angle shot when you return serve. If ball comes to you, not too high so you keep little crook in elbow for stroke, you make nice, *easy cross-court angle shot.* Ball hits side wall near to opponent, goes low to front wall. Even he sees what you do before you stroke, many times opponent cannot reach this angle shot in time. But you need to practice this! Not easy! Delicate touch required!

Other times when you use angle, maybe you need to mask your shot. Maybe opponent watches you very close for early sign of what you do, he wants to run quick to proper place. Do not give such sign, but use body to hide what you have idea to do. Your opponent sees start of stroke—backswing, yes—but he likes to see more. Do not permit. Place body between ball and opponent, so you hide what you do with racquet and wrist for rest of stroke. For one important moment he does not know what you give him—alley shot, cross-court, angle. He does not know where he must go until ball starts from racquet. Now he must run very hard. Maybe his reply is weak! Yes, mask your shot ever you can.

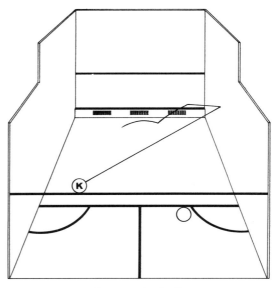

Reverse Angle Shot

Sometime *reverse angle* shot is good idea. For *reverse*, ball goes to side wall most far from you. More difficult than regular angle shot, yes, for reason you must stroke across body to make such big change in direction of ball!

Once in while, perhaps you fool opponent with reverse angle. Example. You are in mid-court, near right wall, opponent little behind you. He sees you begin stroke and way your body turns, he thinks you give him hard, cross-court drive. He turns to run back to far corner. Too bad! You pull ball all way over to far side wall. It bounces to front, and dies. Opponent sees mistake he makes, but too late—he goes in wrong direction!

Sometime you play angle shot from back corner. You try for 3-wall-winner: (1) side wall, (2) front wall, (3)

110

other side wall nick. This shot is gamble, yes. You miss that nick in far wall, opponent has good chance to put away that ball. But if you practice, find where you need to hit side wall, what angle, you begin to hit that nick more times. English have name, *side wall boast* for this angle shot. I like very much for my game. Gamble, yes. Sometime I miss that nick and I have trouble to save point. All right. I try anyway again. You play safe every time, you take joy out of game, my opinion.

other shots?

Other shots? No: alley shot, cross-court, drop, angle, is all I play, all I teach.

True, sometime I use *back-wall boast:* ball passes me, I run after, hit hard and up against back wall. Ball goes high and slow, like lob, to front wall. This is weak shot, forced shot. It does not belong with good shots.

Also, there is *high Philadelphia:* For this shot you must stand in front of court, close to middle. Idea is to pass opponent, when he is close behind you. You hit ball high, very hard to front wall, near corner. This gives high-speed reverse spin. Ball jumps from corner to other side wall, then to back wall. Spin makes ball stay very close to back wall after bounce. If you get such shot from your opponent, do not permit bounce: return hard on volley. I play in Philadelphia city, I have Philadelphia opponents, but never I receive high Philadelphia shot in match! Also, never I give!

Be happy with four good shots!

chapter 7

How I Make Favorite Shots

7

Good friend, also squash student mine, says, "Hashim, give picture of how you win points with certain shots. You are teacher, you teach students to play same like you. Therefore, proper to show shots you make."

I reply, "Shots are not big secret, all good players make same shots."

Friend returns so: "Do all good players write book?"

All right, I decide I do this. And when I think of idea of my friend, I am happy to put together all my shots, I remember more and more and more. I make pictures of near forty shots. I want to forget nothing, I like you to have good bargain in this book.

Later I change, I think maybe you get tired to see all such pictures. More and more I think about some of these shots, more I see they are not so different. Ball hits little different place, yes, but idea is same.

And also I think, "Not necessary to show every shot idea in right-hand and left-hand court!" I show my idea on one side, that is enough. You can see quick how to reverse that shot, change from forehand stroke to back-hand stroke.

Hard I squeeze sponge: many shots run out. Twelve

left. Favorite shot for me. True shots: many times opponents give me such balls in matches, I give them such replies.

You look at all these pictures, you see opponent ever gives me chance to make good shot. Twelve rallies here. I win eleven.

Look like I make myself tiger, opponent tabby cat?

Yes, looks that way!

But how do you learn from Hashim Khan if he makes too many mistakes?

This is reason I most time play properly in Chapter 7.

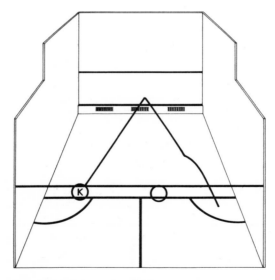

1. On backhand I play very hard cross-court drive to pass opponent, make him run to back corner. But I make mistake: ball goes too low on front wall, bounces in forecourt. Opponent must go back a little, yes, but he makes stroke before ball goes to back wall.

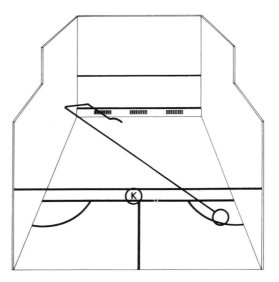

2. *Opponent thinks to end rally with cross-court angle shot. True, even I see his idea before his stroke, I cannot run. First I must permit ball to go. No blocking. Never mind, if angle shot is not perfect, I reach in time. I am lucky, it is not perfect.*

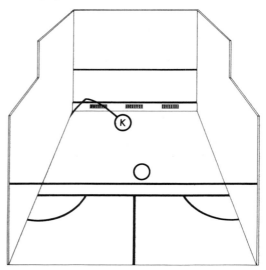

3. *I reach front in time, and play very soft drop shot—front wall, side wall. Ball dies in nick. Not always I do like this: maybe I miss that nick! If I have very fast opponent, and he goes with me like shadow to front, I play other shot!*

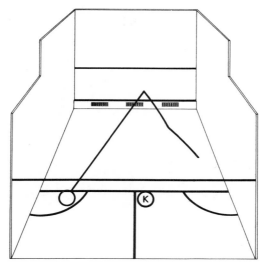

1. I have strong position in "T." Opponent plays cross-court drive to make me leave this place. But ball goes too low on front wall. First bounce is in forecourt. Easy to handle, this ball. Better for opponent if he drives ball more deep in court.

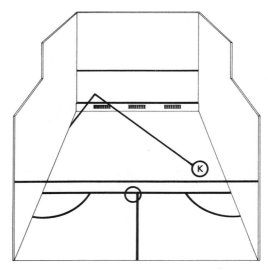

2. I have chance for controlled shot: ball is good height with air all around. I play front-wall, side-wall nick. It is like drop shot, but ball has more pace. To hit nick, I need to send ball medium fast. Without nick, this is weak shot, opponent can reach perhaps. With nick, he never reaches: ball rolls.

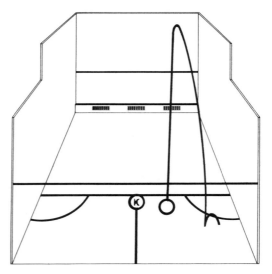

1. *Opponent plays high lob in right-court alley, ball goes far to back before bounce. I cannot volley, mid-court: ball too high in air for good control on stroke. Opponent makes me go to back of court for get. But one small mistake, he makes: ball is out little too far from side wall.*

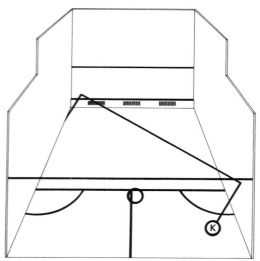

2. *When ball comes off back wall, I try for winner. I stroke hard into side wall: ball flies fast to front wall, then side-wall nick. Important, the nick. When ball hits floor first, it comes up high off side wall. Easy get. Like billiard shot, this one. Necessary to practice angles.*

116

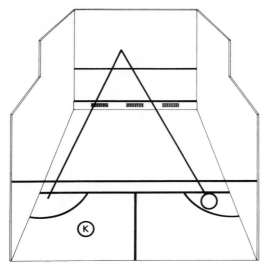

1. *Opponent sends cross-court smash, high on front wall, to pass me. Idea goes in head like electric: "Maybe ball goes to crack in back wall, better I take it in air!" One big step to left, I take, put racquet up quick for backhand get.*

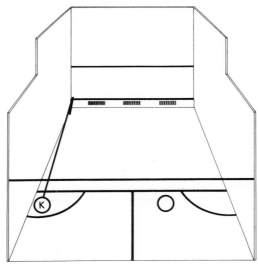

2. *I take that ball in air, before bounce, and send it soft up front, little over tin. Volley drop. Dies quick. Opponent, he is not beginning to run and he loses point. If ball comes to you very fast like that and you want to make drop, give only little baby stroke, just aim that ball to proper place.*

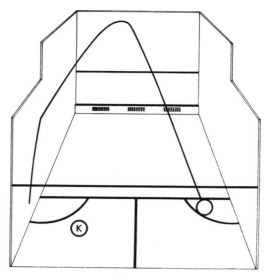

1. *Opponent gives me high lob to my backhand. I can play volley return but ball is not quite right to try for winner. For cross-court angle volley my arm is too straight up for good control.*

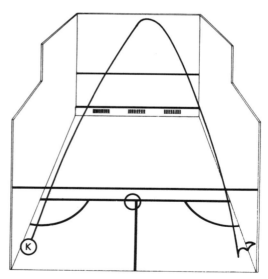

2. *I play safe cross-court lob — high to front wall. Ball bounces in back corner. Opponent cannot catch on volley: he must go to corner. I move to 'T" and watch: does opponent play lob down alley?*

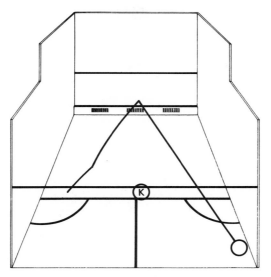

3. No! He thinks to pass me with low, hard cross-court drive. Hits maybe 2 feet over tin. Too low. Bounce is in forecourt. I have chance to reply quick.

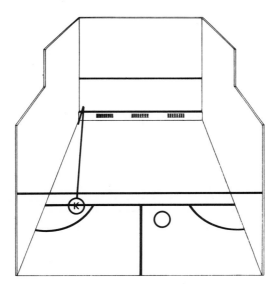

4. Straight backhand drop to front wall, close to side, I play. Soft. Opponent cannot reach. If he plays that cross-court more deep, he has time to move to better position!

119

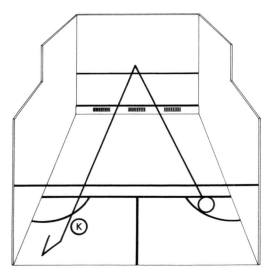

1. *Opponent gives me hammer service, ball flies to me like bullet, it wants to hit me in head. Difficult to make good reply on volley. But if one lets ball go by, does it find crack at bottom of back wall? One must decide! I decide "No!" Yes, correct! Ball bounces on floor first!*

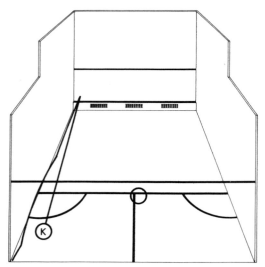

2. *I move to take ball on backhand, off back wall. I play very hard, very low alley shot, move quick out of way for opponent, so he does not say "Let!" Opponent moves fast, thinking to catch ball off back wall. But I hit that ball to bounce twice before back wall. Point!*

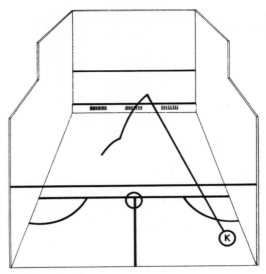

1. *In middle of rally, I play weak cross-court drive from rear. Too low on front wall. This ball never passes opponent: it goes to greet him like old friend!*

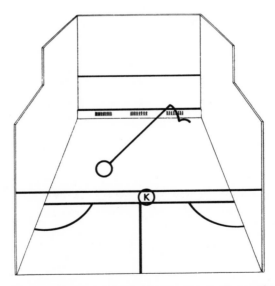

2. *Opponent moves forward, takes ball on backhand. He has idea to play soft drop to right front. Aim is bad. Ball goes too high on front wall. Bigger bounce gives me time to reach.*

121

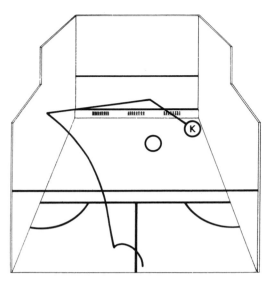

3. *Opponent sees I maybe can make reply, he runs fast with me. I have feeling he is close: better I not play drop shot also. I play hard front-wall side-wall drive. Ball passes opponent, dies in back court. Point!*

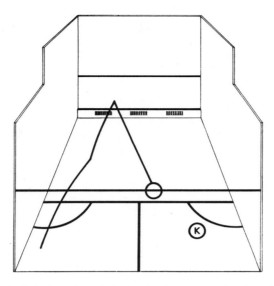

1. *Already he is in front, I am in back, why does opponent make such cross-court drive? Does he think ball dies in corner? Also, why does opponent move up more front to wait for reply? Does he think my backhand is weak?*

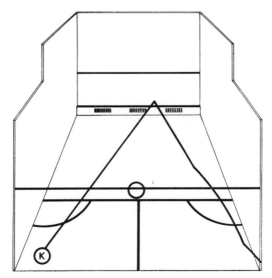

2. *I use full back swing, fast wrist snap, I send ball very hard, very low, cross-court. He is off-balance, my opponent, also surprised. Ball passes him. Point! Student, please remember: always have idea opponent makes good reply, then you are more ready!*

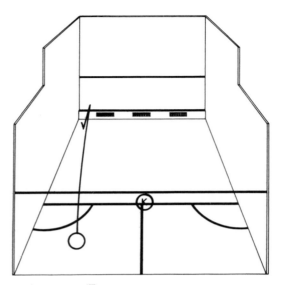

1. *Opponent is daredevil, he is in back, I am in "T." Good idea to send me to*
back with drive or lob, but he plays straight drop! I see his wrist move to
stroke and I begin to move. When ball goes to front wall, I am full speed
on way.

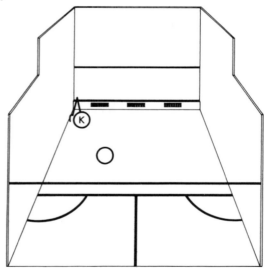

2. *I take last big step and stretch—stretch body, stretch racquet arm out, out,*
out, fast to be in time. I play little soft drop. Better than angle shot for
reason it does not go to center. Dies very quick, this drop. Why does
opponent play drop when he sees I watch him close?

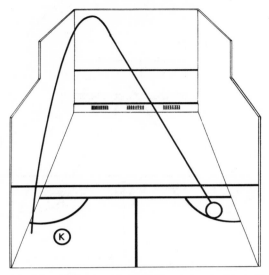

1. *Opponent gives me lob service to backhand. Not perfect, this lob: ball out from side wall, gives me chance to volley. On volley I can play cross-court drop, cross-court angle, but ball pretty high for good control. Better I do something not so difficult.*

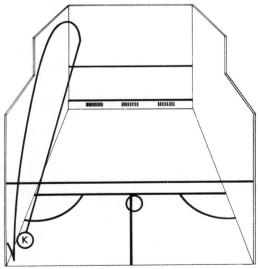

2. *I give him lob also—lob down my alley. Ball goes high to front wall, flies close to back wall before bounce on floor. Opponent must go across court and go to corner to make get. When you know you have not good chance to make a winner, play safe shot: maybe good chance comes next time.*

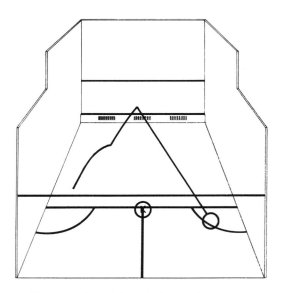

1. *Cross-court drive is good strong attack shot to chase opponent to corner, but ball must have right speed, height. Opponent's shot in picture is too low. Two fast steps and I am ready to stroke.*

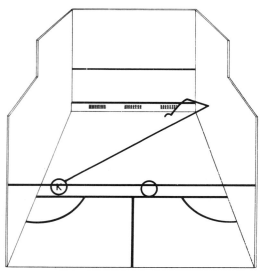

2. *Very easy to play drop near left wall or hard, low alley shot. Never mind, I play cross-court angle — more difficult shot — for surprise. Opponent is off balance and shot is good. Point!*

126

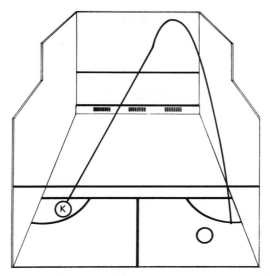

1. *I serve lob, but not perfect: out too far from side wall. Opponent moves to take ball on volley: best idea on lob, if you have chance.*

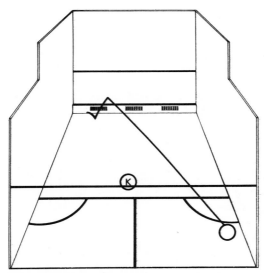

2. *He tries cross-court drop shot. Not safe shot, no, but many time player must take chance to make point. This drop is too far from corner, it comes out in open. On way to front, I see I have chance.*

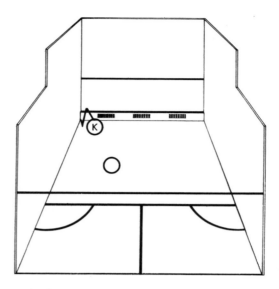

3. I run very hard to play very soft. My shot is drop also, very close to side wall, dies very quick. Most times I win point like this. But when I play such shot against nephew Mohibullah, that is different!

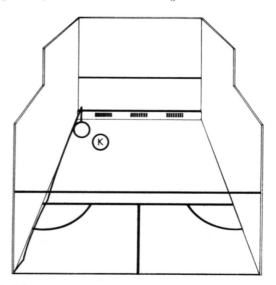

4. Mohibullah is very, very fast. He follows to front and he is there in time for get. He plays hard, low drive down alley. His point! To take point from this young man, necessary you wrong foot him.

chapter 8

Ragout

Different ideas about squash racquets, some advice I have for you, stories I tell you about my experience, they all come together here, in mix. Like little meat pieces, vegetables, spices in *ragout*.

study opponent

Some players have same, every-time opponent pal, they work in same business, they come to play squash together. Sometime I ask such player, "What are strong points, weak points of your opponent?" and he does not know. No surprise for me: I see him in court. Maybe opponent likes to stand near "T" and volley: he is strong in this way. Friend does not watch this, he gives his opponent lovely high balls right in his hand, and opponent enjoys to put away those balls. Friend says, "Good shot, good shot!" It is like he puts head in mouth of lion, he wants to give compliment to lion when he takes bite.

I advise to study your opponent. Every opponent you have, he has his own way to play, different from all other player, it is like different way he writes his name. After few games with him, you know his way to play. You know how to keep head out of mouth of lion. Also how to twist tail.

In beginning, I understand, you cannot study opponent, you have hands full to study self, you try to learn how to stroke, make shots, etc. But later—do not forget!

Sometime you do not need to study opponent to find a weak point. You see it in one moment. One player tells me this helps to win important match for him. He meets opponent first time, and he sees this man has glasses on. So he plays many high lobs, opponent looks up, electric lights in ceiling make flash on glasses, he has trouble to see ball to make good return. Not good sports? You answer! I tell you this: many player I know, professional, amateur, when they want to win match, they do same thing, only they do not tell me about his.

where goes ball?

Every time you see opponent make ready for stroke, you need quick answer for question, "Where goes ball?"

One small moment after racquet hits ball everybody knows answer, yes, of course. But clever player, he is not satisfied like this. He likes to know where goes that ball *before* racquet hits! More soon he knows, more soon he arrives at place where he makes reply. More soon he knows, more chance he has to put body in proper position, make good shot.

Maybe you have experience like this: opponent makes good drop shot, you run hard as can to front, too bad, your racquet is couple inches too late when ball goes to bounce twice. I think maybe you save that point when you see idea of opponent for that drop little more soon. Just *little* more soon: sometime tenth second is enough. You can easy put your racquet one foot more close to ball in tenth second!

How can player know where opponent has idea to send ball before hit of racquet?

Squash student mine tells me old-time American baseball champion Babe Ruth is pitcher in young years, but he has trouble to not tell his idea to batter, every time he sends curve to opponent, he puts tongue out first. He does not know what he does, this is nervous habit.

I do not think you find opponent for squash who does such thing. That is all right. Your opponent cannot help to tell you some of his idea before he hits ball, anyway.

Watch opponent make ready for stroke. Watch how wide he puts his feet, how much he twists his body to wind up, does he look to place where he sends ball. Watch whole man. But most important, watch racquet move for backswing and down-stroke. Racquet or wrist. Wrist I like better to watch for reason it moves little more early than racquet.

You watch opponent like this, I think you catch idea *where* ball goes, *how fast,* maybe half second before hit. Short time, half second, but you need this. Yes, now you know where to go for reply, but you do not jump to this place in one instant. Body does not want to move like this, it takes time. Like big heavy door, it does not move in instant, first you push, then it begins to open.

Yes, important to catch idea of opponent soon as can!

To catch idea quick one thing I learn long time before is most players have favorite shots. They run to certain place in court for get, they make favorite reply. Maybe 3-4 good shots possible to make, never mind, most times they play favorite!

When your opponent runs fast as can to catch ball before second bounce, this is time he plays favorite for sure. No time for him to think, "What shot?" He plays same shot like last time he was in this place, and last time before. He has habit.

Good players, like I tell you before, they study opponent. If they are in court with man first time, they watch very close. In two, three games, they get idea of habit of opponent, they begin to get ready more quick to go to proper place for reply.

Every player I see has some habit, even top players, they like to play certain way in certain places, and always in matches I watch very close in those places for favorite shots.

I give you example. Sometimes in match I make drop shot and it is bad: not close enough to corner, not low enough to tin. Moment that ball goes from my racquet, I know touch is wrong, opponent has good chance for get.

Opponent runs very fast to front. I follow 2-3 steps behind, and keep close to center. I face front, feet wide, weight up front on balls of feet, I am ready to go right, go left, go back.

If I know style of my opponent and he tries very hard to arrive in time for get, I have idea where goes that ball. If opponent is Ray Widelski, I think he hits hard, low drive right down alley. It is favorite for him in such position. Al Chassard, he tries to cross ball from me, to drive it to right hand corner. Vic Neiderhoffer, I watch for him to play cross-court drop to right side. Roshan Khan, I think he plays soft angle shot on left side. And

Henri Salaun, he likes to play safe in spot like this, he gives me lob to send me back.

Remember, never I make move before I am *sure* where goes that ball. I give you favorite shot of some player in one certain position. Maybe I make 2-3 points in match like this. But top players, when they see they lose couple of points with favorite shot, they wake up, they quick make change.

Never mind, to know favorite shot habit of opponent is advantage. Habit is like spring. Opponent pushes away, he makes other shot once in while, but most times habit pulls him back.

Watch your game. Try to keep loose, try many different shots. You keep loose from favorite shot habit, opponent has more difficult time to make reply!

take few lessons

When I go in court with student who is not beginner, he plays few months, I give lesson in two parts. First we have knock-up, I give him balls to backhand, forehand, he hits to me, I watch close, make changes in his stroke, body position, such things.

Then we play some games until he is tired, and this is real lesson. When he makes mistake and gives me ball in hand, I put away that ball. Then we stop game for moment and I say, "Why do you give me bad shot like that?" Most times this bad shot is reflex, he is excited. We start again. Maybe he makes same mistake again. Again we stop and talk. I tell him better shots to make.

This is how we play. What I try to do, is make student *think*. Yes, it is true, he thinks now, but not quick enough to make proper shots. *I put pressure on him to think more quick.*

My opinion, this is best thing coach can do for student.

I put pressure on student to think more quick, make proper shots. You see student mine, John Dunning, fine player, also artist. He makes diagrams for this book.

If you have chance, take few lessons from good coach!

watch to be not hit

Somebody tells me squash player with good stroke makes ball go hundred miles in hour. When you are in way of such ball, you never move self out in time. And when you are hit, I think you hop round for while. Worse than hornet, that ball sting.

All the time watch close to be not hit, quick move after you play to give opponent clear shot. This is good sports.

I do like this and only one time I have trouble, this is one United States Open tournament and I have top amateur for opponent in one match. We play fifth game. I make my stroke, I move quick out of way and all of sudden that ball comes for me, and I am hit. I look at referee. Referee looks at me and gives point to opponent.

Every time now after I stroke, I move more far away. Still I have trouble. One time opponent is in left court, back, I run quick across that court near middle, I stand against side wall. I am hit second time. I hop round and opponent says "Sorry" and referee gives him point for reason he wants to hit side wall where I am standing and I am in way of this shot.

Few moments later, opponent is in back court to take ball, I am near service line. Quick I put myself flat on floor to be not in way. I do not stop on knee like to tie shoe-lace. I go flat — arms, legs straight out like diver.

Zing, I am hit.

I think to ask referee "All right, I jump to gallery to wait for shot of my opponent?" but I am not in United

135

States long time and I do not want people to have idea I am poor sports.

This is only match where ball hits me, and I am sure this is for reason opponent *tries*.

Racquet hit is different. I play this game near forty-five years and never racquet hits me. Never hits me for purpose or in accident.

This is for reason I watch close. Every day when I go in courts with beginners to give lessons, I give plenty of room to them. Sometime they have wide swing. Sometime they lose grip, racquet goes out from hand and flies in air. That is all right, racquet most times you can jump from.

Not just beginner I watch. Everybody. Good players, amateur, professional, they have back stroke, they have follow through. They need some room. Quite proper. I give that room.

No, never I am hit with racquet, but I am sorry to say I hit other persons.

Many years I play with young brother Azam Khan, and many times I hit him. One day he says to me, "Why do you hit people so many times?" like I have joy to do this. I say to Azam, "If you are in way, I am sorry, you are hit."

I cannot help these hits. Always I get my stroke ready early, I make my backswing early, and ever I keep eye on that ball. When ball is coming close, and I start swing, I put whole mind on that ball. Nothing else I see. If opponent comes close, I do not know this. I do not see him, I see ball, that is all, one idea I have is to hit that ball, and when I start stroke, I cannot stop.

If I must all time worry to think, "Where is my

opponent?'' I take my eye from that ball and I cannot hit properly.

One time Azam runs to front to get drop shot I make, and makes drop also. I run to front too and I have idea to play cross-court drive to put ball away from him. Azam does not move out of way for moment. Then he begins to move when I stroke. His foot goes in air and my racquet hits that foot in follow-through. It hits bone in place where shoe strings are. Azam cannot walk properly. We stop. I am very sorry for this.

This accident happens when we play for last point in last game in last match, Scottish Open Tournament, 1957!

Another time, I hit Roshan Khan in quarter finals, United States Open, 1963.

I am making ready to stroke near service line, center, and Roshan is moving to me from left court back. He thinks he knows what I do: he has idea I play soft drop to front right corner, far away from him. He points body to this corner, and he comes close, closer, he does not want so far to run. Not bad idea, drop shot, but I see I can catch him off balance, I can put ball behind his back. I play hard, low cross-court drive to back left corner. But I never finish follow-through, my racquet hits Roshan on back of hand. We stop game and Roshan opens, closes, opens, closes that hand. Numb, that hand—not strong enough to hold racquet. Match is over.

I tell you such stories so you take care. If you forget and come too close, maybe you are lucky, maybe opponent has habit to look around, he sees you, he stops in time. But maybe your opponent is same player like me, he sees one thing only, ball, when he makes stroke.

Watch self! Not rubber, that racquet!

Also, maybe you catch from story of Roshan, when you come too close, you put self out of position, opponent can cross ball to take you off balance, win point easy!

stamina

Many years before, sports newspaper people explain idea why I can run fast for 2-3 matches in same day, never have trouble to catch breath. They say Pathan people (I am Pathan) are tough like leather, they run up and down mountains in N. W. Frontier Province and never they worry about thin air. They say I come down from high place to play in London, other low cities, I never get tired for reason I have much, much oxygen to take in lungs.

Now I tell you fact. Peshawar, city where I learn this game and stay thirty-seven years, is ten hundred fifty feet over sea, that is all. Air in Peshawar is same like air in Edinburgh and Montreal and Seattle.

I know difference when you go high. I have experience like this. Few years ago, Azam, and Roshan and me, we go to Colorado Springs, U.S.A., to play exhibition matches. Before we go, friend tells me maybe I feel something when I run in this city. He says, you drive car here, push gas pedal quick to floor, nothing happens right away, you have to wait little while to go more fast for reason air is thin. I laugh. But true, this story. Air *is* thin, Colorado Springs is six thousand feet more high than sea, highest place ever in world we play squash!

Air Force cadets in gallery, they never know we feel something different up high like that, we play good games. But I tell you truth, these three Pathans from Khyber Pass, we have same trouble like car, we try to go fast, reflex is more slow!

Yes, sports writers make good story for paper. But not right. God gives me good health, good body, I run in court most of life, never I take alcohol, put smoke in lungs, that is true reason I have stamina.

chapter 9

More Ragout

knock-up

Some young players think they get idea about game of new opponent, how he is strong, how weak, in knock-up before match. Sorry, no. Knock-up is just polite way to get muscles ready. Players stand in one place, send ball back, forth, back, forth, right into hand of opponent. They do not run. They take time, make nice, proper strokes, never you learn something like this.

When I go into court with Egyptian Mahmoud El Karim first time, I have idea of his game, yes. I know if I give him ball in right forecourt, I lose rally: he sends that ball hard, low to front wall, it goes to side wall 7-8 feet back, maybe one inch from floor, it is sure kill every time.

Never I give Karim ball in right forecourt, all the time I try to give him ball in back corners. He cannot play his favorite shot.

Where do I learn this information? In knock-up? No. In knock-up I learn nothing. English professional tells me this before match.

doubles

Not very much doubles squash racquets I play. It is like different game, and never I learn best ideas how to win. Ball is more lively, court is enormous, and I cannot use wrist to make shots same way as regular squash game. Elbow must go out from body, and I take more wide stroke for distance, like tennis.

In 1964 nephew Mohibullah and I go to Toronto and we are lucky to win Canadian Open Doubles Match. Next year we go back and we lose to two fine players, Sam Howe III, Philadelphia, and partner Bill Danforth, Pittsburgh. We have some small difficulty to decide in court who runs for each ball, Mohibullah or Hashim. Not lazy, both happy to run, but one at time is enough!

In winter 1966 we try again in North American open for doubles. This time we have little talk before we go in court, we decide what balls belong to Mo, what are for me. We win this match.

be not nervous

One man takes phone to call friend, says, "You like to play game?" Friend replies, "Great idea!" They smile when they come together, slap each other on back. They go in court — run, jump like crazy, they laugh at mistakes, they say compliments to opponent for good shots, they try to win from other but loser stays happy. They enjoy game.

Now, make change. Same men go in same court, but now is not friendly little game. It is match in tournament. There is referee in gallery and some few people come to watch.

These men enjoy to play now? Many times, no. They feel little weak. Stomach is not happy. Brain does not want to work. They hit ball too soon, too late, ball goes crooked out from racquet. But they never laugh.

Nervous, these men! Many players I see like this,

141

I have students now, they play good as can in friendly game, but they go in regular match, they make one hundred mistakes! I tell them: "You are stiff like board, let loose your body. Do not worry to lose. Just do best you can."

Once in while, player is lucky, he gets to be not nervous in match. Most times when he starts to be nervous, he never changes, always he is nervous in match.

Top squash racquets players maybe be a little nervous before match, yes. They think, "I need idea how to win from this opponent," stomach shakes, they do not like to eat. But there is big difference when game begins. They do not worry. They play. And it is truth, they play best games of life. It is like they want to show people in gallery some good shots, they want those people to have joy in game also. And when the people clap their hands after good rally, this makes them feel strong, they are happy, never nervous.

If you are scared of match, maybe you need some practice. Do not care to win for while, go in court to learn. Take time, no hurry, play many many friendly game, also play by self. After while, I think you play pretty good even you do not feel very good...even you are worried ...even you are scared. Now maybe you are ready to put name down for tournament! I think you be not nervous!

can game grow?

You ask question, "Can game of squash racquets grow?" Look at Australia, you find answer.

First time I visit on exhibition tour, 1952, one big city where I play, Sydney, has 8 squash courts only, all private club courts. Five years go by, I visit again, 1957, and now, amazing, Sydney has *four hundred courts*, with lockers and showers and small charge for anyone to play! Yes, they are public. Some of these courts I see have meter like taxi, you pay by clock.

Next year, 1958, I go third time to this country, I play Frank Sedgeman (champion tennis player and good friend) in Australian Professional Match, and now in Sydney and villages in New South Wales, they have total *four hundred fifty* public squash racquet courts!

To build one court takes — $10–15,000 I think. With this you can have small house. Most countries, sports people shake their heads, they worry to know where they can find such money.

In Australia, they do not worry, they build those courts, and players pay for them!

"trick" shots

Sometime in game I cannot help to have bad position. Ball comes fast, near left side of me. I face front wall. No time to turn. I quick put racquet *behind my back* to catch that ball. I push stomach out and make body in shape like bow to give room for little swing, and I stroke that ball.

Once in while, good cross-court lob passes me, I cannot volley, that ball is too high. I run to back. Ball comes very weak off back wall, near corner. No room for proper swing. Now I make bad shot, but what can person do? I face backwall, crouch down low, send ball back over head to front. Slow it goes, yes. Maybe opponent makes kill shot now? Maybe. I watch and see.

143

Some time ball comes quick to back side of you, no time to turn. I quick swing racquet behind back and stroke that ball.

You see bad shot, but what can person do? Ball comes very weak off back wall, near corner. No room for swing. I face back wall, crouch low, send ball back over head to front.

Sometime I am face to front wall, when ball comes low, fast, straight to me. No time to change position. That is all right, I make shot between legs. When you try this, be careful. Just small swing.

Sometime I am in front and I face to front wall when ball comes low, fast straight to me. No time to change position. That is all right, I put that racquet *between legs* and make shot. Not big swing: dangerous for self with this shot.

From early years I see people in gallery laugh to see such shots. They have idea it is entertainment, tricks. Never I have such idea. I am out of position, I play like this for reason I can do nothing else. Anyway, I enjoy to make the people laugh.

Laughing gallery is main idea for man like Amin Khan, third cousin mine. He is squash professional in Ceylon, I think (*was* in Karachi) good player, but in top rank never for reason he likes too much to eat and is too big for running. But beautiful shots he has, and many many tricks. Gallery laughs and claps for Amin like I never hear before.

Young nephew Mohibullah watches Amin very close in Pakistan and he takes couple of tricks for self.

One is for laughing only. Ball comes to Mohibullah medium high. He takes big, big back swing, strokes hard as can. What happens? He misses! That is all right, racquet keeps going, going, goes behind back, and Mohibullah catches that ball at end of follow-through, with hand behind back! Sometime gallery is too serious and he is few points ahead in game, Mohibullah plays this trick to make people laugh.

Other trick is like this: Mohibullah is near front to make easy get of slow ball. He takes time, turns head to look at one corner in front. You watch his eye, you think he picks out exact place in this corner where he sends that ball. Opponent, he cannot help to look at this corner also,

145

and maybe he starts to move this way. Mohibullah strokes, but that ball goes to *other corner* for nice soft drop or angle shot!

Ever you go in court with Mohibullah, do not watch his eye, watch his wrist! Also, better you do not take this trick for your game. Keep eye on ball!

game for women?

Never in my country women play this game of squash racquets. It is not custom, also not permitted by religion for women to show face outside house to stranger. And I even do not see British women in Pakistan play when I am young man, but I see many later when I go to England.

Most time on exhibition tour I give lessons and one time in Australia I give some few lessons to woman, name of Miss H. Blundell. Already when I meet her, she is good player. Later she becomes British Women's Open Champion, I think 6 times! She is big, strong, good stamina, she strokes and runs and plays shots like man, I am surprised. I give lessons to some few other women in different countries, but Miss H. Blundell is best woman student.

I do not think it is good idea, woman playing squash with man opponent, for reason she has handicap: she is not so strong in wrist and arm, and cannot twist quick to change direction like man. Not fair match. Better women play only other women.

Also, I believe British game better for women than American game. In American game, they have trouble to

146

control the ball, it is too hard, too fast. English game they play nicely.

poor behavior

Some squash racquets players, they think they have trouble to win regular way—fast running, good shots, quick think—they get idea to take mind of opponent off game to make weak his play. Then they have better chance.

When I am referee in small city matches I see such thing many times.

One man I watch, ever he has match with new opponent for first time, he goes in court to look like he is just healing up from accident. Never I see stretch bandage like this. He has stretch bandage on elbow, on knee, on calf of leg, on thigh. Also he wears wrist band, sweat band around head and, once in while, small plaster on face. Truth!

He walks very careful into court for knock-up, like he is afraid to strain some hurt. Opponent's eyes go big to look at him. I have idea he thinks: "Maybe this man hurts self bad if I make him run too fast!" He likes to win, yes, of course, but this poor bandage man has handicap—not fair! He gives himself handicap, he sends easy shots into hand of bandage man, he lets him take lead in this match. Later, he thinks, I take lead back. Sorry. Bandage man, never he has real hurt anywhere, he runs like crazy to keep that lead, many times he takes that match!

Another man I see likes to give idea he hurts self

147

when he has hard time in match. Maybe his opponent makes 4-5 points in row, this opponent gets everything, makes beautiful shots, it looks like nothing stops him. Good time for this man to hurt self.

He runs for get, all of sudden he falls down to floor. He rolls back, forth, back, forth, holding tight to leg. Some couple of people go in court, they feel leg to see is bone broken. If doctor is in gallery, he goes in to feel also. No, bone all right, muscle hurts. After five minutes man stops the roll, he sits up to rub that leg. Couple more minutes he stands up, he puts some weight on that poor leg, now he walks little. In fifteen minutes he likes to play again and everybody goes back to gallery to watch.

Opponent? Before, he has joy in game, he hits ball well. Now he feels cold to game. He feels angry, he thinks this man fools him, but he can say nothing, this is poor sports. He cannot put all mind on game now, he makes mistakes, he loses that lead, maybe he loses match!

Such tricks like this, I laugh to see one moment, then next moment I think, "It is bad for game, poor behavior." Never I see first-class player who tries to win like this.

gamesmanship

There is quiet way to break concentration of opponent, quite all right, so many people try to do this. There is special name, gamesmanship. I give you example.

Few years ago Mr. Edward Hahn plays Mr. Donald Legatt in finals of Hamilton Invitational in Canada. Very close, this match. It is fifth game, score is tied 17-17 and Don Legatt steps in box to serve.

Now like I tell you before, Don Legatt has smashing cannonball service. He throws ball in air, he leans back to start big overhand stroke, when all of sudden he stops. Mr. Hahn is saying something to him. He says "Watch your foot." Then he turns to gallery and says to referee, "Watch his foot."

Mr. Hahn does not say Don Legatt's foot goes out of service box on serve before. Just very polite he says "Watch foot."

Don Legatt never watches foot same time he serves before, never any player does this, anyway he worries so much that his foot can leave box, he makes mistake on hard serve, and ball flies up in gallery! One fault.

Don Legatt is very, very careful on second serve. He does not take chance with another cannon ball. He gives soft easy ball to Mr. Hahn. Too bad. There is short rally, and he loses point, he loses game, match, whole Hamilton Invitational!

Don Legatt laughs, he is good sports.

Sometime I try little gamesmanship, I fool opponent how I feel. If I feel not good, have trouble to run, never I say this. If opponent hears such thing, it is gift to him, it makes him more strong, he knows he has better chance to win.

One match I feel bad, that is truth, and I never think and talk too much about condition. But I am one lucky man: this one time this talking helps to win!

January 1963 I am in Montreal for Canadian Open, and I feel worse and worse. I have flu bug when I go there, I sneeze, go hot, cold, nose leaks, so on; and in last game of quarter finals, I am in court with Douglas McLaggan, and I pull muscle in small part of back. Never I say anything, I try to keep pain away from face and I finish that match.

Next morning, good friend, he brings me red lamp to shine on back, but this does not help quick enough, and I take codeine pills to be not careful with the pain when I move in court. This codeine and aspirin I take for flu, they are not happy in stomach, and I feel like I am better in bed when I go in court with Henri Salaun for semifinals in afternoon of this day. But never I say anything!

I try very hard and I win that first game. Mr. Salaun never he says to me how *he* feels, but I see in long rally he gets tired too quick. He does not wait in court one minute to start play again, he goes out of court, he walks into shower, then he puts on all fresh clothes, top and bottom, he is gone one long time. Referee says nothing, I say nothing, I fool Henri Salaun, he does not know I need very bad this rest also.

He comes back in to court and this second game *he* wins, and again he goes out for the shower and dry clothes and no person says anything, and he comes back and we play and this third game Henri Salaun wins also.

We go out from court. Now I know I have five minutes rest for sure. It is rule after 3 games, and I hope Henri Salaun takes long time again.

I sit on bench in locker room and think, "How do I win fourth game?" and this man comes to me — I do not give his name — and asks how I feel and I say to him truth, "I feel worst of my life, I am very tired." Later I find out this man goes to Salaun and says, "Better you go quick back in court, you finish off Hashim, he is sick man."

Quick, before five minutes is over, Salaun comes to me and says, "You ready to play?"

150

All of sudden I am angry with self to sit and cry like baby, I do not care any more how feels my back, my stomach, I say "Yes, I am ready!" and we go in court and I am like different man, I put whole mind on game, and I win this match!

chapter 10

Good Condition and Strong Attack!

It is good idea to finish this book now, I believe, so I make this chapter last chapter. Already I tell you story of my life. I give information for beginners in this game. And for experienced player, I show some ways I learn to win points. I like to give you big fat book to read, but better I do not say many times same thing.

It is true, it does not take many pages to put down all important ideas about squash. Forty-five years I have racquet in hand, and what I learn goes on one page.

Keep eye on ball.

Move quick to "T."

Stay in crouch.

Take big step.

Keep ball far away from opponent.

Have many different shots ready so opponent does not know what you do next.

Do not relax because you play good shot; maybe opponent retrieves that ball; better you get ready for next stroke.

Soon as can, find out where opponent has idea to send ball, then quick take position for your return shot.

Have reason for every stroke you make.

You can put these ideas in your head in a few

minutes, yes. Now, you learn to make these ideas belong to you, you remember them in court, never you need anything more, they give you good games all your life!

Perhaps you look for more ideas, *different* ideas? Perhaps you think, "All good players have same such ideas as Hashim Khan puts down." Perhaps you think I have special ideas I learn in court and keep for myself like special way some cook has to prepare curry, and I can give them to you here.

Sorry, no ideas like this. All good players I meet in court everywhere, North America, Europe, Asia, Africa, Australia, they all have same ideas how to hit ball like me. When somebody says before match, "Look out, I discover new shot, you never catch that ball!" they make joke. Squash racquets is same now like in time of my grandfather on stone courts in Peshawar. Rules change a little. Rubber in ball is better. Racquets improve, yes. But game? Same!

Yes, unfortunate I have no big secrets for finish of my book. Anyway, I give you two ideas, not new, old ideas, two ideas I think help me win matches. Perhaps you like to take them for your game.

One idea is good condition to play hard. The other idea I have is strong attack.

good condition

Myself I am lucky to have good condition from early age. From time I am boy eight years old I go in the courts every day. Never I stop to think what I do, but I learn to breathe deep, always I try to suck in more air so I can stay running. I grow big chest, much room for air, and with rest of body small and light. I am like little car with large petrol tank, I can go long time and never stop.

Also I have excellent opponents from beginning, this is important. Maybe you learn yourself, you think you are in shape but then you play much better man, and you see you must run more fast, you cannot get your breath, you think then you are in terrible shape. Well, for myself, I am lucky to learn this game in Pakistan, this is a country of tennis and squash racquets players, and always I can find first-class games.

Every year before I go to London to play in English Open, I work very hard with first-class players. For 4-5 hours every day in Peshawar I run with Azam Khan, Roshan Khan, Safirullah Khan, young nephew Mohibullah, such players, also other excellent players of my country. It is like training camp. To win is hard work!

When time comes to go to England, I am in excellent shape, and this is one important reason I win matches.

Many times my opponent has not chance to train very hard like this. Yes, he gets weight down. He plays many good games getting ready, but perhaps his opponents do not make him run and think hard as can. They do not *stretch* him. Also, maybe he likes to slow down a little after hard rally, and opponent likes this also.

When I go in court with him, never I take slow-down if I feel good. Pressure I keep on. Opponent is in very good condition. Yes, he does not have trouble to catch breath. But many times, after while, I see change. He does not leap like before to make gets. His timing goes off a little. His drives are not so hard like in beginning. He does not think so fast.

Of course, I am a professional and for a professional condition is very important. It is a shame to have poor condition, for then one cannot properly make living. For amateur it is different, squash racquets is a game for fun only, he has other way to make a living, he is doctor, lawyer, salesman, accountant. When condition is not top, he has excuse.

strong attack

So condition is one reason I win, and I believe other reason is strong attack. These ideas belong together, you cannot have one only. Impossible to play kind of game I like, attacking game, if condition becomes weak in court. But I am fortunate to have top condition for many, many years. Therefore, I attack.

I like to finish quick. Ever I try to stay in front of opponent. Yes, of course, he tries to make that ball pass me, but then I jump, I leap, I run fast to take that ball early on volley or perhaps half-volley, and if I have position for some control I put that ball so opponent must try very hard for get. I speed game up. I make it go fast as possible to end of point, win or lose. Opponent has no time to get set. All time he is running, twisting, jumping. All time he has pressure. Pretty soon in this rally, maybe I catch him off-balance so he makes very weak return, then I play winner.

When opponent makes good shot and thinks I have difficulty to make satisfactory return, he thinks I will be happy to make careful, safe return, no problem for him, maybe this is time I try for winner. Yes, I gamble, I take chance. I do not care to play up-court, down-court many many strokes, waiting for opponent to make some mistake, so I can get cheap point. I try quick as possible for kill. Maybe I make mistake myself, yes. Of course. Many times I hit tin, I miss that crack. This is gamble, this is joy game. When I start to have fear to make mistake, then I think I am ready to stop this game!

I do not want to talk like I am proud man. I tell you such things about me so you can understand why I win matches. Maybe they help your game!

This is truth: more you know about this game, better you play, then you have more pleasure from it. Every player I ever see has idea to do better, some take lessons from me, some just watch good players and take their ideas this way. No matter, they go in court with friend: If they come out winner, fine, it is keen good feeling, they are sure they improve. If they come out loser, too bad, they are some unhappy, but they tell themself, "I know mistakes I make, next time I do better!"

I hope you find some help in this book. I hope you have much joy in this wonderful game, squash racquets!

Keep eye on ball!

appendix

championships of hashim khan*

Year	K's Age**	Event	Place	Final Opponent	Scores
1944	28	Western India	Bombay	Abdul Bari	Unknown
1945	29	Western India	Bombay	Abdul Bari	Unknown
1946	30	Western India	Bombay	Abdul Bari	Unknown
*1947					
1948					
1949	33	Pakistan Prof.	Kakul	Safirullah Khan	9-1,9-4,9-1
1950	34	Pakistan Prof.	Kakul	Safirullah Khan	Unknown
1950	35	Scotland Open	Edinburgh	Mahmoud El Karim	9-2,9-0,9-4
1950		British Open†	London	Mahmoud El Karim	9-5,9-0,9-0
1950		British Prof.	London	Abdul Bari	9-4,9-7,7-9,8-10,9-3
1951	36	Scotland Open	Edinburgh	Mahmoud El Karim	9-0,9-0,10-8
1951		British Open	London	Mahmoud El Karim	9-5,9-7,9-0
1951		British Prof.	London	L.W.R. Keeble	9-3,9-3,9-3
1952	37	Scotland Open	Edinburgh	Azam Khan	Unknown

Year	K's Age**	Event	Place	Final Opponent	Scores
1952		Dunlop Prof.	London	Mahmoud El Karim	9-3,9-3,9-7
1952		British Open	London	R.B.R. Wilson (Am.)	9-2,8-10,9-1,9-0
1952		British Prof.	London	Azam Khan	9-6,4-9,9-7,5-9,9-6
1953	38	Scotland Open	Edinburgh	Azam Khan	8-10,9-5,9-3,8-10,9-3
1953		British Open	London	Azam Khan	6-9,9-6,9-6,7-9,9-5
1953		British Prof.	London	Azam Khan	5-9,9-6,7-9,9-5,9-7
1954	39	Scotland Open	Edinburgh	Azam Khan	9-7,9-10,9-3,3-9,9-5
1954		British Open	London	Azam Khan	9-7,7-9,9-7,5-9,9-7
1954		British Prof.	London	Azam Khan	7-9,9-6,8-10,9-5,9-6
1955	40	Scotland Open	Edinburgh	Azam Khan	10-9,7-9,9-7,9-5
1955		British Open	London	Roshan Khan	9-4,9-2,5-9,9-5
1955		United States Prof.	New York	Azam Khan	18-16,12-15,16-18,15-4,15-9
1955		Pakistan Prof.	Peshawar	Azam Khan	
1956	41	Scotland Open	Edinburgh	Azam Khan	9-7,7-9,9-5,9-7
1956		Pakistan Prof.	Karachi	Roshan Khan	Unknown
1956		United States Open	New York	Roshan Khan	12-15,15-5,15-3,15-9
1957	42	Scotland Open	Edinburgh	Mohibullah Khan	10-8,9-5,10-8
1957		British Open	London	Azam Khan	9-7,6-9,9-6,9-7
1957		Australian Open	Adelaide	John Cheadle	9-1,9-6,9-7

158

Year	No.	Tournament	Location	Opponent	Score
1957		Australian Prof.	Adelaide	Roshan Khan	9-2,9-1,9-1
1958	43	Dunlop Prof.	London	Azam Khan	9-7,10-8,9-7
1958		Australian Prof.	Melbourne	Frank Sedgman	9-5,9-5,9-6
1960	45	Canadian Open	Toronto	Mohibullah Khan	(3 Games to 1)
1962	47	Canadian Open	Toronto	Al Chassard	(3 Games to 0)
1963	48	Canadian Open	Montreal	Mohibullah Khan	(3 Games to 2)
1963		United States Prof.	Boston	Al Chassard	15-12,15-10,15-7
1963		United States Open	New York	Mohibullah Khan	15-6,10-15,15-10,11-15,15-12
1964	50	Toronto Pro-Am Invitational (Doubles, with Mohibullah Khan)	Toronto	Al Chassard Ray Widelski	(3 Games to 1)
1966	51	North American Veterans Prof.	Toronto	Frank Iannicelli	15-9,15-5,15-8
1966		Toronto Pro-Am Invitational (Doubles, with Mohibullah Khan)	Toronto	Samuel P. Howe R. William Danforth	15-9,15-12,15-8
1967	52	North American Veterans Prof.	Milwaukee	Frank Iannicelli	15-4,15-6,15-6

notes

*This record of Hashim Khan's Championships throughout the world, since he entered formal match play in India in 1944, has been compiled by Arthur B. Sonneborn. Despite persistent enquiry, in a few cases the precise match results in game scores or number of games played remain unknown.

For the benefit of readers who may be puzzled by the difference in British and American match scores, we give the explanation:

British Scoring. The British game is a nine-point game. Points are made only on Hand-In, which means the server is the only one who can score. If the score becomes 8-All, the player who is not serving may either elect No-Set, which means the first player to reach nine wins the game, or he may choose two, in which case the player who scores two more points wins the game.

American Scoring. The American game is a 15-point game. Either player may win a point, which means that he does not have to be serving. The player who first scores 15 points wins the game, excepting that:

(A) At 13-All, the player who has first reached the score of 13 must elect one of the following before the next serve: (1) Set to 5 points, making the game 18 points; (2) Set to 3 points, making the game 16 points; or (3) No set, in which event the game remains at 15 points.

(B) At 14-All, provided the score has not been 13-All, the player who has first reached the score of 14 must elect one of the following before the next serve: (1) Set to 3, making the game 17 points; (2) No set, in which event the game remains 15 points.

**A running record of Hashim's age is included, as of interest, since he entered top-level competition relatively late, and scored his most impressive victories at ages when the stamina and drive of most players show signs of waning.

†Because the court is larger, requiring more movement, and the ball less bouncy, requiring more speed in retrieving, the English game has been generally considered as somewhat more demanding of stamina than the American game. And in the English game, the British Open, in which the best amateurs and professionals from the Isles and the Commonwealth nations compete, has been regarded as the most gruelling test of a player, and a tournament win the highest achievement in the sport. It is, in effect, the World's Championship.

For these reasons, and because he was 35 when he first competed and was generally playing against younger men (brother Azam, for instance), Hashim's seven British Open Championships ('50, '51, '52, '53, '54, '55, '57) is an awesome record. It has never been equalled. Hashim competed on two other occasions. He pulled a shin muscle and was forced to retire in the finals match against cousin Roshan in the '56 Open; and in the '58 Open twisted his knee and was unable to continue, in the semi-finals against brother Azam!
R.E.R.

Hashim Khan is Professional at the Uptown Athletic Club, Detroit.

Richard E. Randall is a graduate of the University of Michigan. He has spent many years in the communications field, principally as writer and producer. His latest position is that of Associate Director, TV-Radio, D. P. Brother and Company.

The manuscript was prepared for publication by Ralph Busick. The book was designed by Donald Ross. The typeface used for the text is Linofilm Palotino designed by Hermann Zapf in 1950.

The book is printed on P. H. Glatfelter's Offset paper and bound in Interlaken's Pallium cloth over boards. Manufactured in the United States of America.